Ed Gorman and **Simon Pearson** are both journalists and published authors. Ed is a veteran news and war correspondent, who worked for *The Times* for 25 years and who recently published an autobiographical memoir, *Death of a Translator*. Simon is a journalist and author who worked for *The Times* for more than 30 years. He wrote *The Great Escaper*, a biography of Roger Bushell, "Big X" of Stalag Luft III, which was published by Hodder & Stoughton in 2013 and became a top-10 bestseller.

Battle of Britain

The Pilots and Planes
That Made History

SIMON PEARSON
AND ED GORMAN

HODDER

First published in Great Britain in 2020 by Hodder & Stoughton
An Hachette UK company

This paperback edition published in 2021

I

Copyright © Simon Pearson and Ed Gorman 2020

The right of Simon Pearson and Ed Gorman to be identified
as the Author of the Work has been asserted by them in accordance
with the Copyright, Designs and Patents Act 1988.

A CIP catalogue record for this title is available from the British Library

Paperback ISBN 9781529378085
eBook ISBN 9781529378108
Hardback ISBN 9781529378061

Typeset in Bembo MT Pro by
Palimpsest Book Production Ltd, Falkirk, Stirlingshire

Printed and bound in Great Britain by
Clays Ltd, Elcograf S.p.A.

Hodder & Stoughton policy is to use papers that are natural, renewable
and recyclable products and made from wood grown in sustainable forests.
The logging and manufacturing processes are expected to conform
to the environmental regulations of the country of origin.

Hodder & Stoughton Ltd
Carmelite House
50 Victoria Embankment
London EC4Y 0DZ

www.hodder.co.uk

In memory of
RJ Mitchell
Aeronautical engineer
1895–1937

For Fi
with love

Contents

Introduction

T HE FULL STORY of the Battle of Britain has been told many times. Our purpose, on its eightieth anniversary, is to bring to life the pilots and planes involved through the stories of eighteen airmen – nine from each side – and eighteen different aircraft.

We have chosen pilots from seven nations: Germans, Britons, two New Zealanders, two Swiss, a Canadian, a Pole and an Italian. Men from many other countries were also involved in the battle. The ranks of Fighter Command, like Nelson's navy at Trafalgar and Wellington's army at Waterloo, were truly cosmopolitan. The combatants included American volunteers, Australians, Belgians, Czechs, Free French, Irish, Rhodesians and West Indians. Pilots from Austria and South Africa fought on both sides.

Many of our featured pilots are not well known, which gave us the chance to shed light on their lives, their suffering and their remarkable stories, in a number of cases for the first time. For some chapters we were lucky enough to find comprehensive accounts of the lives and loves of the men involved. In others, we had to make do with far less information, but we resisted the temptation to fill in the gaps with better-known characters. Several of our pilots died in action, others spent years in captivity. A few of them suffered terrible wounds, while many survived remarkably unscathed, physically at least.

What most, if not all, of these men had in common was a love of flying, courage in the face of formidable odds, and a willingness to take risks that are unimaginable for those of us whose only flying experience consists of the comfort and safety of commercial jet travel. Each pilot's story reminds us of the extraordinary adventures these men were undertaking at a time when death was often a matter of a moment's loss of concentration.

The book also features a variety of aircraft: like the pilots, we have chosen a wide range, among them the four-engine Focke-Wulf Condor and the Fiat CR42 biplane fighter on the Axis side, and the Boulton Paul Defiant fighter with its rear turret and the Walrus seaplane on the Allied side.

Some aircraft were superstars in their own era – the Spitfire and the Messerschmitt Bf 109, for example – but almost all of them represented considerable achievements in engineering, design and manufacture. One or two, like the Defiant and the Stuka, were 'found out' in the testing cauldron of the Battle of Britain. Others proved their worth and flew throughout the war, as new marques were developed.

Today, the Battle of Britain continues to fascinate historians and the general public. Some regard it as the last chivalrous battle to have been fought. But while there was undoubtedly some kind of bond between the pilots, perhaps their shared joy of flying, it was a brutal encounter in which few favours were granted.

The significance of the battle is sometimes downplayed because of the relatively few lives lost on each side – 3,149 all told – in a global conflagration during which far greater numbers were killed in a single day elsewhere. Yet casualty figures and the strategic significance of the Battle of Britain should not be confused.

During the summer and autumn of 1940, some people referred to the skies above southern England as the 'Burning Blue', a battle-field unlike any other. In those skies, men from many nations, flying predominantly in the uniforms of the British and German air forces, decided the fate of the world.

It was that simple. Had the forces of Nazi Germany prevailed, Britain would in all likelihood have been invaded. Had it been conquered, Adolf Hitler would have been free to wage war elsewhere, unencumbered by an enemy on his Atlantic doorstep.

Britain survived, however, and even before the battle was over, its armed forces were reinforcing its presence in Africa and the Mediterranean, and Winston Churchill had formed the Special Operations Executive, which would attempt to wage a covert war on the Continent. Indeed, Britain became the launch pad for the eventual liberation of Nazi-occupied Europe in the west and a bulwark against Soviet expansion.

The Battle of Britain proved to be a turning point – a moment in time that, like Waterloo, would define the country's history and sense of itself for most of the subsequent century.

Britain won the battle because of the leadership of three men: an eccentric Englishman with few friends, a canny and determined New Zealander, and a bull-like Canadian. Air Chief Marshal Sir Hugh Dowding and the New Zealander Air Vice-Marshal Keith Park had a plan and they stuck to it despite opposition from their own side.

The Canadian Lord Beaverbrook, a key ally of Churchill's, transformed aircraft production in Britain, and made sure that Dowding and Park had the Spitfires and Hurricanes they needed to see their plan through.

Once the Germans had conquered France, they moved 2,500 Luftwaffe bombers and fighters to upgraded airfields on the Channel coast – but they did not have a plan for fighting a strategic air battle. Unlike his RAF counterparts, Reichsmarschall Hermann Goering, the head of the Luftwaffe, changed his tactics at critical moments. Several of Goering's most senior generals were indulgent and incompetent. Among them was Hugo Sperrle, the commander of Air Fleet 3, who failed to co-operate with Albert Kesselring, who commanded Air Fleet 2.

The Battle of Britain called for a new strategy, but none was forthcoming; there were few conferences and no staff studies. The Germans had more sophisticated radar than the British, but they failed to understand the importance of Britain's radar network. The Germans had better combat pilots, many of them veterans of the Spanish Civil War, but they lost the cream of these because their flawed intelligence system failed to recognise the strengths and weaknesses of Fighter Command.

The one thing that the Luftwaffe and its commanders had in spades at the start of the battle, however, was confidence. But much of that was misplaced – with irreversible consequences for the Third Reich.

The commanders of the RAF, Dowding and Park, created the first integrated air-defence system in the world, which used the new technology of radar, thousands of observers and a control and command system that enabled them to get their fighters into the right places at the right times to confront their enemies.

With every year that has passed since 1940, the importance of trying to preserve and present the stories of the pilots and planes involved in the Battle of Britain has become more acute. In this book you will not find a day-by-day account of this epic aerial encounter between Britain and Germany, but a sequence of portraits of men and machines – some that are not usually associated with the battle – fighting on either side between 10 July and 31 October. Taken together, we hope these stories shed new light on this extraordinary period of European history and make a small contribution to its bibliography.

Simon Pearson and Ed Gorman

Key Dates

1935

26 February: Nazi Germany acknowledges the existence of a military air force, the Luftwaffe, with Hermann Goering as its commander-in-chief, in defiance of the Treaty of Versailles.

1936

5 March: The Supermarine Spitfire makes its first flight.
14 July: Air Chief Marshal Sir Hugh Dowding is appointed head of RAF Fighter Command.
1 August: A German military unit known as the Condor Legion, equipped with many of the country's latest aircraft, is sent to Spain, where pilots and crews gain invaluable combat experience, flying in support of the nationalist forces of General Francisco Franco.

1938

The first five Radio Direction Finding Stations – now known as radar – become operational in southern England. They are a key component of the Dowding System, the first integrated air-defence system in the world.

1939

3 September: Britain and France declare war on Germany after the Nazi invasion of Poland two days earlier.
16 October: German aircraft bomb targets in Britain for the first time.

1940

18 March: Alan Turing's code-breaking machine, 'Bombe', which will eventually allow the British to read Luftwaffe signals traffic, is installed at Bletchley Park in Buckinghamshire.

9 April: Germany invades Denmark and Norway.

10 May: Germany invades France and the Low Countries; Winston Churchill becomes prime minister of Great Britain.

15 May: RAF launches its first big raid on Germany, with 99 aircraft attacking targets in the Ruhr.

26 May – 4 June: Operation Dynamo – the evacuation of nearly 340,000 predominantly British troops from Dunkirk.

18 June: Churchill tells Parliament that the Battle of France is over, and that the Battle of Britain is about to begin.

2 July: Adolf Hitler orders his armed forces to prepare for Operation Sealion, the invasion of southern England.

10 July – 11 August: First phase of the Battle of Britain starts as the Luftwaffe tests British defences with attacks on shipping in the Channel and ports.

13–23 August: Second phase of the battle starts with what the Luftwaffe calls 'Eagle Day', with formations bombing targets across the country, including radar stations and the RAF's forward bases.

15 August: Dubbed 'Black Thursday' by the Luftwaffe, which flies 1,786 sorties – the most on any day of the battle – with heavy losses.

20 August: Speaking in Parliament, Churchill immortalises Fighter Command's pilots as 'The Few'.

24 August – 6 September: Critical period for the RAF during third phase of the battle as the Luftwaffe targets RAF fighter airfields in the south-east.

24 August: German aircraft bomb central London for the first time.

25 August: RAF bombs Berlin.

7–30 September: Luftwaffe attacks focus on London, first by daylight, then by night, heralding the start of the Blitz and the bombing of cities across Britain.

15 September: Luftwaffe bomber fleets mauled. *The Times* declares: 'RAF Batter Invasion Machine'.

17 September: Hitler postpones invasion of Britain indefinitely as it becomes clear that the Luftwaffe has failed to establish air superiority over southern England.

31 October: Last day of the Battle of Britain, but the Blitz continues.

14–15 November: Two thirds of the industrial city of Coventry is laid waste by 515 German bombers, led by a pathfinder force using radio beams to find the target. The cathedral is destroyed. More than 500 people lose their lives and 800 more are injured.

29–30 December: The 'Second Great Fire of London', when St Paul's Cathedral – captured in a famous photograph – stands undamaged amid the smoke and fire.

1941

10 May: The Blitz ends with the 71st raid on London, which kills 1,436 people. Across Britain, 44,652 had lost their lives, with 20,292 injured as a result of the Luftwaffe's campaign. More than four million people were evacuated from their homes or displaced.

22 June: Nazi Germany launches Operation Barbarossa, the invasion of the Soviet Union.

A Junkers 87 dive bomber attacking a British ship in the Channel during the Battle of Britain. The German aircraft, popularly known as the Stuka, had been a potent weapon in Poland and France

I

First Lieutenant Karl Henze
Junkers 87 Stuka Dive Bomber

14 July 1940

His aircraft was seriously damaged.
He also had a bullet lodged in his skull.

THE BATTLE OF Britain is chiefly remembered through the written accounts of those who fought in it, surviving official records, snippets of film, and as a result of the many photographs of aircraft on the ground, often with their pilots, or in the air. One of the most remarkable sources, however, is a radio broadcast that went out on the BBC on 14 July 1940, by the reporter Charles Gardner. This has been preserved in its entirety.

Gardner had gone to Dover to try to capture in real time the dramatic events in the Channel, as the Luftwaffe stepped up its attacks on Allied shipping using the Strait of Dover during the first phase of the battle. This lasted a month and was called *Kanalkampf* – 'Channel War' – by the Germans.

Among the German pilots involved in these operations was Karl Henze, who flew a Junkers 87 dive bomber or Stuka, one of the Luftwaffe's most feared aircraft. Henze was highly trained and had already been decorated for his role in the campaigns in Poland and France, but even for an experienced pilot, it was difficult to hit a ship from the air.

Gardner watched as the action began to unfold within sight of his clifftop position, where he had a panoramic view out to sea.

He was not the only figure to broadcast about the war that Sunday. In a radio address, Churchill declared that Britain would fight on alone: 'But be the ordeal sharp or long, or both, we shall seek no terms, we shall tolerate no parley; we may show mercy – we shall ask for none.'

Some hours later, Gardner described a series of attacks on a British convoy as a formation of Stukas targeted ships protected by three RAF Hurricanes from 615 Squadron.

'The Germans are dive-bombing a convoy out to sea,' explained Gardner, who sounded rather breathless. 'There's one going down on the target now . . . bomb! No! He missed the ships. It hasn't hit a single ship. There are about ten ships in the convoy, but he hasn't hit a single one.'

In the background of his report, guns can be heard firing close to him. 'And . . . there, you can hear our anti-aircraft going at them now,' he continued. 'There are one, two, three, four, five, six – there are about ten German machines dive-bombing the British convoy, which is just out to sea in the Channel.'

Then Gardner described the RAF's response. 'I can't see anything. No! We thought he had got a German one at the top then, but now the British fighters are coming up. Here they come. The Germans are coming in an absolute steep dive, and you can see their bombs actually leave the machines and come into the water. You can hear our guns going like anything now. I am looking round now. I can hear machine gun fire, but I can't see our Spitfires. They must be somewhere there.'

The reporter went on to describe what he thought was a German pilot bailing out of his Stuka, whereas historians believe this was Michael Mudie, a British Hurricane pilot from 615 Squadron. He was picked up by a Royal Navy vessel, but he died the next day from wounds he had sustained in the fighting.

'Oh, here's one coming down,' was how Gardner reported it. 'There's one going down in flames. Somebody's hit a German and he's coming down with a long streak, coming down completely out of control . . . a long streak of smoke. And now a man's bailed out by parachute. The pilot's bailed out by parachute. He's a Junkers 87, and he's going slap into the sea . . . and there he goes. Smash! A terrific column of water and there was a Junkers 87 . . .'

The broadcast, which was distributed in shops as a 78 rpm gramophone record to raise funds for the war effort, was a highly unusual live account of aerial warfare. It was controversial then and it remains so; Gardner often sounds as if he is commentating on a football match rather than on mortal combat over the Channel.

Yet his report also provides a vivid contemporary account of the Stuka in action. At the time, this was the world's most successful dive bomber – one in which the twenty-four-year-old Karl Henze was distinguishing himself as a German combat pilot – but one that would quickly prove disastrously vulnerable in the unique conditions of the Battle of Britain.

The dive bomber was intended to act as a form of long-range artillery in support of ground troops and tanks spearheading the Wehrmacht's concept of Blitzkrieg, or 'lightning war'. The Stuka needed to be strong, agile and accurate. For pilots like Henze, dive-bombing was hugely demanding, both mentally and physically; they had to fly on an almost vertical trajectory towards the ground to deliver a bomb and then pull out at the last minute, when they would often – quite briefly – lose consciousness.

The Stuka's origins go back to the early 1930s, when Colonel Ernst Udet, a German fighter ace from the First World War, was visiting the United States. While there, Udet saw a Curtiss biplane known as a Helldiver. He was impressed by its characteristics and potential, so without arousing American concerns about his intentions – the planes were already regarded as obsolete – he purchased two of the aircraft and had them shipped back to Germany.

Erhard Milch, the Secretary of State at the Ministry of Aviation in Berlin, saw the potential in this type of aerial weaponry, and he invited the Junkers aviation company and several other manufacturers to produce prototypes. The Junkers conception, which initially had a twin tailplane – replaced by a sturdier single fin after early trials – was an ugly, functional-looking wasp of a plane with an angular fuselage. It featured low-slung gull wings fitted with air brakes, a glazed cockpit for the pilot and rear gunner, and fixed wheels with distinctive aerodynamic fairings around the undercarriage.

Designed by Herman Pohlmann, the Stuka – or *Sturzkampfflugzeug*, meaning dive bomber – started rolling off the production line in 1936. Like some other German prototypes of the time, an early version flew with a British Rolls-Royce engine. This was replaced by a Junkers Jumo power unit as the aircraft evolved through many iterations. The Stuka had a top speed of 230 mph in level flight

3

– making it one of the slowest aircraft committed to the Battle of Britain – and it could carry one sizeable bomb or up to four smaller ones. It was armed with two machine guns in its wings and one or two machine guns for the gunner/radio operator seated behind the pilot.

In the dive procedure, initiated through a complex series of actions by pilots such as Henze, the aircraft would go into a vertical descent travelling at up to 370 mph. A bomb would be released at about 1,500ft using a swinging crutch to send it clear of the propeller. The plane would then pull out of the dive using an automated control mechanism, which was necessary because at this stage the pilots would be under intense stress caused by the g-forces exerted on them.

Perhaps the most famous characteristic of the Stuka was its fearsome howling as it went into its dive before the pilot released his bomb. This screech was generated by small propeller-driven sirens known as Jericho Trumpets mounted on the leading edge of the wings or on the undercarriage. These sirens terrified men and women on the ground even before the Stuka's bombs had landed and are thought to have been proposed by Udet – or Hitler.

Later models did not carry sirens because they affected the aerodynamics of the plane, slowing it down by up to 20 mph. Instead, some bombs carried by Stukas were fitted with whistles that produced a similar effect.

In the build-up to the Second World War, like many other new Luftwaffe aircraft, the Ju 87 was tried out in the Spanish Civil War. It evolved through a series of often dangerous test flights, which included one of the Luftwaffe's worst air disasters. In August 1939, shortly before the invasion of Poland, fourteen Stukas were sent up at Neuhammer to demonstrate the plane's prowess to visiting generals. Before the Stukas started their dives, cloud conditions changed and ground fog swept over the airfield. As a result, the pilots began their steep descent too close to the ground. The fourteen planes crashed, killing all but two of the twenty-eight aircrew.

The Stuka came to the Battle of Britain after winning its spurs in Poland, where it had been used to devastating effect and where Henze won the first of his many gallantry awards, including the Iron Cross, both 1st and 2nd class.

Karl Henze flew more than 1,000 missions in Stukas, many in Russia, and was highly decorated

Stukas were involved in the first air raid of the war – against the town of Wielun between 4 and 5 a.m. on 1 September – and it was a Stuka that achieved the first German air victory, when Lieutenant Frank Neubert shot down a Polish fighter while it was taking off from Balice airfield, killing its pilot, Captain Mieczyslaw Medwecki.

The Ju 87 was also used to great effect in the Norway campaign, where it was deployed in a ground-attack role in support of the army and against shipping. The strategy continued during the Battle of France, especially at Dunkirk, when Allied troops waiting to be evacuated from the beach proved easy targets for marauding Stukas dropping fragmentation bombs.

All indications were that the Stuka would be a potent adversary in the Battle of Britain, and in the beginning, squadrons of Ju 87s successfully attacked convoys in the Channel. On 4 July, for example, four freighters were sunk in one convoy and six others were damaged. Later that day, Stukas sank the 5,500-ton anti-aircraft ship HMS *Foylebank* in Portland harbour. One of the British casualties, Leading Seaman John Mantle, was posthumously awarded the Victoria Cross for continuing to fire on the German dive bombers after being severely wounded as his ship sank.

But then the Stukas began to suffer huge losses, even when they were escorted by Messerschmitt fighters. It quickly became obvious that while the Stuka was a devastating weapon after air superiority had been achieved – as had been the case over Poland and France – it was hopelessly vulnerable to enemy fighters. The aircraft was simply too slow and poorly armed to compete with a Spitfire or Hurricane. The Ju 87 was particularly vulnerable when it came out of a dive and when its pilots were heading home across the Channel in level flight. They often flew low, trying to avoid detection, but were shot down in large numbers.

In *The Battle of Britain* by Kate Moore, the decorated Hurricane pilot Flying Officer Geoffrey Page says that the Ju 87 had become almost too easy to shoot down. 'Don't forget after the Stukas pulled out of their dive at sea level, they had to fly back to France, at about 10ft above the waves,' he said. 'In our Hurricanes, by throttling back the engine, we could sit behind the Stuka and there was the poor rear gunner with just one pop gun to defend his aeroplane, while we were sitting there with eight machine guns. They were a pretty easy target and I'm not proud of the fact that one just knocked them off like skittles.'

On 13 August, Stukas attempting to bomb Middle Wallop airfield in Hampshire were bounced by Spitfires from 609 Squadron and nine were destroyed in a few minutes. Within six days, forty-one Stukas had been lost and by 18 August the Luftwaffe had to withdraw the dive bombers from the battle. The decision was made after two disastrous deployments. On 16 August, nine Stukas were shot down during an attack on Tangmere airfield in Sussex; two days later, sixteen were destroyed when they attacked the airfields at Ford and Thorney Island, also in Sussex.

It was during the attack over Ford airfield that Henze so nearly became another fatality of the Battle of Britain. Instead, he would go on to become one of the most prolific Ju 87 pilots of the Second World War, amassing an incredible 1,098 missions by April 1945.

On 18 August, Henze came within a few feet of death over the Channel. By that stage he was one of the Luftwaffe's most experienced Stuka pilots and may well have been one of those described so memorably on BBC radio only a month before. During the raid on Ford, Henze's plane was badly mauled during a clash with RAF Spitfires. The hydraulics on his aircraft were seriously damaged. Henze also had a bullet lodged in his skull.

Despite the damage to both pilot and plane, Henze managed to struggle back across the Channel, although he was in danger of being shot down at any moment. At one point he is thought to have touched the waves with his broken undercarriage before wrestling his Stuka back into level flight. After reaching the French coast and crash-landing north-west of the ancient town of Bayeux, he was treated for his wounds. He did not fly on further military operations until 1941.

Born in January 1916 in Holzminden, south of Hanover, Henze joined the Luftwaffe in 1936. He took part in the invasions of Greece and Yugoslavia and in Operation Barbarossa, the attack on the Soviet Union. He flew in the siege of Sevastopol on the Crimean Peninsula, when the Luftwaffe flew thousands of sorties against the Red Army and the Black Sea fleet, and during the decisive defeat at Kursk in the summer of 1943. He is said to have saved one downed aircrew from behind enemy lines while under heavy fire. He was shot down several times but, remarkably, always survived.

Henze was decorated many times and in July 1942 became one of only 882 men to receive the Knight's Cross of the Iron Cross with Oak Leaves, an award for extreme bravery on the battlefield or successful military leadership.

By the end of the conflict, Henze had been promoted to the rank of major. He was taken prisoner after surrendering to Allied forces on 8 May 1945 – the last day of the war – but was released by the British on 10 October that year. He joined the postwar German air force in 1956, and retired as a colonel in September 1970. Little appears to be recorded about his private life.

He died at Neunkirchen-Seelscheid in Germany on 25 September 1985 – more than forty-five years after Charles Gardner's famous account of the attack on British shipping by the vaunted Stukas.

And although that aircraft proved unsuitable for the Battle of Britain, it continued to be developed – 6,500 were built – and deployed during the remaining years of the Second World War.

Clem Hunkin was a studious and rather humble man from South Wales who, in 1940, was the pilot of a Wellington bomber. He was also trained by British military intelligence to write secret codes

2

Pilot Officer W.H.C. 'Clem' Hunkin
Vickers Wellington 1A Long-Range Bomber

18 July 1940

*He set in motion events that would undermine
the Third Reich for five years.*

As THE LUFTWAFFE was attacking British shipping in the Channel, the RAF was looking for ways of hitting back at targets in Germany. Although Bomber Command is rarely acclaimed for its role in the Battle of Britain, it flew thousands of sorties in the months from July to the end of October, and lost more men than Fighter Command.

On 18 July 1940, a Vickers Wellington twin-engine bomber at RAF Marham was loaded with 4,000lb of explosives, which were destined to be dropped on an industrial target in the German city of Bremen.

On this occasion, however, the pilot of the Wellington carried a far more potent 'weapon' in his head and he would soon set in motion events that would undermine the Third Reich for five years, long after the aerial battles that raged over Britain in 1940.

Pilot Officer W.H.C. Hunkin – christened William Henry Clement, but known as 'Clem' – was a studious, rather humble man from South Wales, who had been educated at Neath Grammar School for Boys. He had a big smile that revealed his craggy teeth, but, with hooded eyes set under thick brows and a heavy mop of brown hair, he could appear quite sinister.

In the spring or early summer of 1940 – the precise date is not known – Hunkin became one of a handful of airmen serving with Bomber Command who were selected for special training by MI9, a branch of British military intelligence. As he flew over the North Sea on that July evening, Hunkin must have been aware that he might soon be called on to use the skills he had learnt from MI9.

His aircraft was one of sixty-eight bombers dispatched to six targets in Germany, including Hamburg, Essen and Bremen. The raid was one of many flown by 115 Squadron as British bombers targeted the German aircraft industry and Nazi transport and communications links, often deep inside the Third Reich.

Hunkin's aircraft was a high-performance bomber – the best available to the RAF at the time – with an innovative airframe designed by Barnes Wallis, the scientist, engineer and inventor of the bouncing bombs that would be used by the 'Dambusters' of 617 Squadron in 1943.

While Wallis's airframe gave the Wellington great strength, the aircraft remained vulnerable to the increasingly formidable German air defences. Indeed, Bomber Command, which flew 9,293 sorties during the Battle of Britain, would lose 307 of its aircraft in combat and crashes.

One of those aircraft was lost on the night of 18 July. Hunkin's Wellington is believed to have been hit and badly damaged by anti-aircraft fire while he attacked an airframe factory in Bremen. Yet Hunkin successfully crash-landed his bomber near the village of Klein-Henstedt, south-west of Bremen.

Photographs of the downed bomber still exist; the fuselage is broken in two, with the latticework of its geodetic construction exposed in several places, and the rear gun turret is badly smashed. The wings appear to have been sheared off.

Remarkably, all six crew members survived – Pilot Officer Joseph Baker, who was Hunkin's co-pilot; the observer Sergeant C. Clark; and three air gunners, all sergeants, J.J. McGregor and A.G.S. Colley, who doubled as wireless operators; and H. Dickson.

After escaping from their aircraft, the British airmen took refuge in a barn, but were discovered and handed over to the Luftwaffe, which was responsible for all Allied airmen who became prisoners of war.

On the same day, after a long period of silence during which he hoped the British would make peace, Hitler addressed the Reichstag in Berlin. There he made a final appeal. The Nazi leader denounced

The wreck of Hunkin's aircraft after it was shot down near Bremen, and a flight of Wellington bombers

Clem Hunkin with Jean on their wedding day

Churchill and promised 'unending suffering and misery' for the British unless they saw reason and made peace. His 'offer' was rejected.

For the growing number of Allied airmen falling into German hands, it would be a long war.

Hunkin was taken to Dulag Luft, an interrogation camp about four miles north-west of Frankfurt on the outskirts of Oberursel, on 20 July. When it opened in December 1939, Dulag Luft consisted of one white stone building, with a large, steep roof, and housed the first RAF officers to be taken prisoner. In 1940, three wooden barracks were built and the stone house was used only for interrogating prisoners.

The commandant was Major Theo Rumpel, a veteran intelligence officer, who was a charming, cultured man, with a long angular face, blue-grey eyes and a friendly smile. He spoke perfect English and used charm and guile as weapons of interrogation. He was good at his job.

On arrival, Hunkin was stripped and given overalls, while his uniform was searched for escape aids such as compasses and maps. He was then put in solitary confinement.

The pilot, aged only twenty, was visited by German interrogators during the first twenty-four hours and presented with a bogus Red Cross form. This required him to answer far more questions than were stipulated under the Geneva Convention, which provides rules concerning the treatment of prisoners of war. While the forms issued at Dulag Luft asked legitimate questions, they included others about domestic matters such as marital status, and requested military details about the prisoner's squadron, types of aircraft, station and station number, plus the names of crew members and their fate.

Most men refused to answer questions other than their name, rank and number, but some were duped and Rumpel built up a bank of helpful knowledge.

Prisoners whom the Germans did not consider valuable as potential sources of information were usually moved within a few days to permanent camps in Germany or elsewhere in occupied Europe. Those suspected of withholding useful intelligence would remain in solitary confinement at Dulag Luft for further questioning.

Hunkin gave nothing away – and aroused no suspicions. He was given the PoW number 125.

Hunkin's mother, Minnie, who lived in Neath, was told in a telegram from the Air Ministry that he had been shot down. A letter followed on 22 July, which she is likely to have shared with Clem's three elder sisters, Kathleen Mary known as Molly, Anita and Joan.

The letter from the Air Ministry said:

> I am to explain that this does not necessarily mean that he is killed or wounded and that if he is a prisoner of war, he should be able to communicate with you in due course. Meanwhile enquiries will be made by the Air Ministry through the International Red Cross Society. As soon as any definite news is received, you will be immediately informed.

Minnie Hunkin's son left Dulag Luft twenty-four hours later. But in the three days that he had spent at the camp, he transformed the ability of prisoners of war to aid the Allies.

After his interrogation by the Germans, Hunkin was questioned by senior British officers, who formed a small permanent British presence in the camp and liaised with the camp commandant, Rumpel. Hunkin was interviewed – if not at first, certainly later – by Wing Commander Harry Day, the Senior British Officer in the camp, and his right-hand man, Squadron Leader Roger Bushell, who was head of the escape committee and responsible for gathering military intelligence.

'Wings' Day, as he was known, a forty-two-year-old pilot shot down flying a Blenheim light bomber on a reconnaissance mission in October 1939, and Bushell, a Spitfire pilot shot down over Boulogne in May 1940, would become the most influential characters in captivity. The two men went on to wage war from within enemy territory – and Hunkin provided them with a new weapon: secret codes through which to communicate with London.

According to the official history of Dulag Luft, written by British officers after the war and marked Top Secret: 'The existence of an official code was not known until the Spring of 1940. The first P/W to arrive in this Camp who could operate this code and had been registered [with MI9] before he became a P/W was: 42231

F/Lt W.H. HUNKIN, RAF – who reported to the Senior British Officer that he knew the code. The Senior British Officer had a Hugo's French pocket dictionary and with the aid of this HUNKIN taught the code to several other P's/W.' The report can be found in the National Archive.

The code was called 'Amy', and it was one of several given to MI9 by Foreign Office code experts. These enabled messages to be hidden in routine letters to friends and family, which the prisoners were allowed to write every month. The key to the code was found in the pocket edition of Hugo's French dictionary.

MI9 had been born out of the experience of the First World War, when the War Office eventually realised that prisoners of war – both British servicemen held in German camps and Germans held in Britain and France – were a potential intelligence asset that, with the right handling, could provide information on issues such as troop movements and enemy morale.

The organisation was formed on 23 December 1939, and operated from Room 424 at the Metropole Hotel, a few hundred yards from the War Office. Its main activities would be two-pronged: aiding the means of escape and promulgating the transfer of intelligence about Germany, starting with details about Luftwaffe interrogation techniques and culminating in information about the country's secret weapons programmes.

MI9 was headed by Norman Crockatt, a forty-five-year-old former soldier, who had been highly decorated and badly wounded on the Western Front during the First World War. He believed that prisoners remained an active force; a 'fighting man remained a fighting man, whether he was in enemy hands or not', and he had a duty to continue fighting in captivity.

The organisation targeted British officers who appeared to be bright, responsible and discreet and who could further its aims if they fell into enemy hands. Pilot Officer W.H.C. 'Clem' Hunkin was such a recruit – and he remained at the heart of MI9's operations for the rest of the war.

His mother first heard that he was alive through a German radio broadcast on 24 July, which was confirmed in a telegram from the Air Ministry three days later.

His first letter home – at least the first we know about – was addressed to an uncle, Mr L. Edwards, at the Midland Bank in Lydney, Gloucestershire. It was dated 31 October and reads:

> I have written to the British Legion, asking them to send me parcels, which will be debited to my account – I have also written for some maths books.
>
> Wonder if you could attend to these small matters. Hope all is well with you and your family and best wishes, Clem.

This letter is uninhibited and the writing flows.

On 14 December he wrote to another uncle, Arthur Rayner Jones, at his mother's address. His letter reads:

> My dear Rayner, Thank you for your letter. I hope that you are all well, and that you manage to leave the old rut occasionally, and head home fast. My home coming is nearer I hope. When it's here we'll be able to exchange our experiences for hours together – with some beer to sit over. We shall have a wizzard [sic] time. Am studying especially hard at present working steadily at a language at last! Having never been an expert at them it is growing more difficult – have to exert myself a lot and manage it. All the best, Clem.

This letter is very different in style and tone; it feels almost stilted and may well have contained a coded message. We may never know.

The official history of the camp is clear, however: 'The dispatch of messages was organised by BUSHELL, DAY and HUNKIN' and they 'used the code from July 1940'.

At first MI9 had difficulty identifying coded letters, but the organisation then worked more closely with the families of prisoners known to be its 'agents' in the camps; it also made improvements to its code-writing craftwork to keep correspondence secret from the Germans.

After leaving Dulag Luft, Hunkin was taken to a permanent camp, Stalag Luft I, on the Baltic coast, where he continued to organise and engage in code work. A year later, he was joined there by Day and Bushell, both of whom had been recaptured after organising the first mass escape of the war by RAF officers – from Dulag Luft.

In 1942 all three men would – by various routes – find themselves at Stalag Luft III, the Luftwaffe's high-security camp at Sagan,100 miles south-east of Berlin. Determined to make life as difficult as possible for their captors, Day and Bushell organised what became known as 'The Great Escape' when, on the night of 24 March 1944, seventy-six Allied officers broke out of the camp. Three made it back to Great Britain, but seventy-three were recaptured and fifty were shot dead by the Gestapo on Hitler's orders.

While at Stalag Luft III, Day and Bushell also expanded the gathering of military intelligence and, with Hunkin at the heart of operations, ramped up the coding. As Crockatt wrote after the war: 'Our codework grew to such an extent that it was obvious a special section had to be formed to deal with the volume of work.' He set up a codes and communications unit to tackle the task.

The fate of the three men who started coding at Dulag Luft in 1940 was very different. Bushell was one of the fifty men shot by the Gestapo. Day, who also took part in the escape, was recaptured but survived the war. After more than five years as a PoW, he returned home to a hero's welcome and was awarded the Distinguished Service Order for his actions in captivity.

There is no record of Hunkin having taken part in an attempted escape from any of the camps in which he was held, but he was probably considered to be too useful as a prisoner organising and writing coded letters.

He left Stalag Luft III in January 1945, when the Germans marched thousands of Allied prisoners westwards in the face of the Russian advance in the east. Hunkin was liberated that May and returned quietly to Britain, where he was reunited with his mother, Minnie, and his siblings, almost five years after he was shot down.

Hunkin's father, Harry, who ran a butcher's shop in Neath, had died of pneumonia at the age of forty-seven in 1928. Clem's sister Molly had also contracted pneumonia, but she survived.

Minnie was left to bring up her four children on her own, but managed to do so in relative security. In 1938, after grammar school, Clem joined the RAF as an officer cadet, and was promoted to acting pilot officer on 20 July 1939. He was promoted to flight lieutenant while he was in captivity, in December 1941.

After being demobbed in 1945, Hunkin read engineering

(Mechanical Science Tripos) at St Catharine's College, Cambridge, for a two-year post-service degree. He later joined Rolls-Royce in Derby before moving to the Bristol Aircraft Corporation at Filton, near Bristol.

At about the same time he married Jean Davies, a local girl from Neath, and they moved to Thornbury in Gloucestershire. Hunkin's nephew David Jones, who also studied at Cambridge and would later become a life fellow in engineering at Christ's College, recalled visiting the couple as a boy.

'I must have been nine or ten,' he said, 'and Clem took me to see Britannia aeroplanes being assembled in the "Brab Hangar" at Filton. Much later, in 1966, on the way back from a Glamorgan Youth Orchestra visit to Czechoslovakia, our chartered Britannia landed at Filton, where Clem introduced me to their chief metallurgist; I had chosen to read materials science as my third-year subject at Cambridge.

'He also took me to see the Concorde engine slung beneath the bomb bay of a Vulcan bomber, which was used as a flying test bed for the engine. I remember seeing pieces of telltale cord lightly glued to the upper leading corner of the engine nacelle, to determine air-flow patterns.'

Hunkin left Filton to become the managing director of a French company manufacturing aerospace bearings. He was responsible for setting up the operation at a factory near the M4, south-west of London.

The stress of the job and the fact that, like so many former airmen, he was a heavy smoker, probably led to his premature death. He had a heart attack at the wheel of his company car in 1974. He managed to get to the hard shoulder and stop, but he was found dead in his seat. He was fifty-four.

It is not known whether anyone represented the intelligence services at his funeral at St Mary's Church, Thornbury, but the turnout was huge.

The intelligence operation triggered by Hunkin's knowledge of code Amy provided extensive information about Germany from a number of sources, including the observations of prisoners coming and going from various camps, Luftwaffe camp staff who were bribed and interrogated by British officers, and from 'friendly'

German sources – both military and civilian – who were hostile to the Nazi regime. Indeed, the prisoners were a major source of intelligence in Germany, second only to the famous Enigma code-breakers at Bletchley Park.

As far as we know, Hunkin never talked about his 'secret war', and his work was not recognised, publicly at least. After all, he had been, to all intents and purposes, a spy working in breach of the Geneva Convention.

Like Hunkin, the Vickers Wellington served throughout the war, and was the only British bomber to do so. Armed with up to eight Browning .303 machine guns and carrying a bomb load of 4,500lbs, the crew of six could fly 2,500 miles at a top speed of 235mph. More than 11,000 Wellingtons were built in several variants, which served in many theatres of operations, most notably with Bomber Command. The aircraft was used in more than 47,000 wartime raids, with 1,332 lost in action. Characterised by its deep girth, the Wellington was popular with its crews, who dubbed it 'the Wimpey', after a portly character from the Popeye cartoons.

The Heinkel 59 of the German air-sea rescue service saved the lives of many Allied crews as well as those of Luftwaffe pilots, but had a wider role in the Battle of Britain

3

First Lieutenant Erich Chudziak
Heinkel 59 Seaplane

27 July 1940

*He was barely eight days at the front when he
was shot down over the English Channel.*

O N 14 JULY 1940, the RAF issued a communiqué that was to
have a profound impact on Pilot Officer Erich Chudziak and
the crew of his Heinkel 59 seaplane.

The instruction to British fighter pilots in Bulletin 1254 declared
that German air-sea rescue aircraft, painted in white with clear red
crosses and operating during the Battle of Britain – and in some
cases saving the lives of RAF pilots – were to be shot down.
Explaining the order, the communiqué said: 'Enemy aircraft bearing
civil markings and marked with the Red Cross have recently flown
over British ships at sea and in the vicinity of the British coast, and
they are being employed for purposes which His Majesty's
Government cannot regard as being consistent with the privileges
generally accorded to the Red Cross.'

The reason for this controversial decision, which divides historians
and specialists on the subject to this day, was that Fighter Command
had discovered what it believed to be firm evidence that the Heinkel
59 seaplanes used by the German air-sea rescue service were not
non-combatants, as the Luftwaffe claimed.

The Germans complained that the new order was a clear breach
of the laws on warfare laid down by the Geneva Convention. But
intelligence sources suggested that the planes were being used to
monitor Allied convoys and that the information was being relayed
back to fighter and bomber squadrons. Further evidence was found

in a downed He 59 pilot's logbook; this indicated that he was collecting information on targets. Radio listening posts also identified He 59s flying in areas where no combat had recently taken place. It suggested that the Heinkels' true purpose was reconnaissance.

Churchill later added another reason to attack the German seaplanes when he wrote: 'We did not recognise this means of rescuing enemy pilots who had been shot down in action, in order that they might come and bomb our civilian population again.' The Germans accused him of committing 'war crimes'.

Initially the Luftwaffe did not change the appearance of its planes and they continued to operate as before, but the relatively slow and old-fashioned He 59 seaplanes proved to be easy targets for RAF fighters, even if some pilots had reservations about attacking them.

There are conflicting accounts as to whether Chudziak, a German, and his crew were shot down on 27 or 28 July, but it is the former that is recorded on his memorial plaque. After the He 59 took off for the last time, the aircraft was flying about ten miles north-east of Dover when its presence was detected by the British early warning system. At 6 p.m., two sections of Hurricanes led by Squadron Leader Joe Kayll were scrambled from 615 Squadron at RAF Kenley and ordered to investigate.

According to his combat report, they came across the German seaplane flying alone at 500ft and, in a series of attacks by pairs of Hurricanes, the aircraft was forced down to sea level. 'E/a [enemy aircraft] burst into flames and Red 2 (Hugo) had one burst into e/a which crashed into the sea,' reported Kayll, who became an ace during the Battle of Britain. 'The e/a was white with large Red Cross [sic] on top of wings, red band on fuselage and Red Cross on fin or rudder.'

When the aircraft went down, Chudziak and three other members of his crew – Ernst Melzer, Josef Baumueller and Willi Paddags – were killed. Only the radio operator, Josef Buess, was picked up and survived. Two days after Chudziak's death, the Luftwaffe ordered all He 59s engaged in air-sea rescue to be armed and repainted as normal frontline aircraft.

Even by the standards of 1940, the He 59 was an old-fashioned beast and one of only two machines featured in this book that did not have enclosed cockpits for its pilot and crew. A biplane and

A German airman standing by a Heinkel 59, and the memorial to
Erich Chudziak on the island of Sylt

WER UNTER DEM SCHIRM DES HÖCHSTEN SITZT UND UNTER DEM
SCHATTEN DES ALLMÄCHTIGEN BLEIBT / DER SPRICHT ZU DEM
HERRN:
MEINE ZU-
VERSICHT U.
MEINE BURG,
MEIN GOTT,
AUF DEN ICH
HOFFE

Erich Chudziak

geboren am 2. Mai 1910 in Gelsenkirchen.
gefallen am 27. Juli 1940
Seine Ehefrau ist Thea Chudziak,
geborene Sch-üler.

Erich Chudziak war Oberleutnant in einer Seenotstaffel. Er
war kaum acht Tage an der Front, als er mit seiner Maschine
am 27. Juli 1940 über dem englischen Kanal abgeschossen
wurde und in treuer Pflichterfüllung den Fliegertod starb.

SIEHE / ICH WILL EINEN
NEUEN HIMMEL UND EINE
NEUE ERDE SCHAFFEN /
DASZ MAN DER VORIGEN
NICHT MEHR GEDENKEN
WIRD.

seaplane, it was one of the first new aircraft built in Germany after the Treaty of Versailles and, like many other projects intended for use in the military, it was initially disguised as a civilian passenger transport aircraft. But its real purpose was as a maritime bomber or reconnaissance aircraft.

Designed by Reinhold Mewes and built by Ernst Heinkel, it featured a large and angular box-like fuselage, with twin engines set between the wings and two floats underneath the wings in which the fuel tanks were housed. The plane had three open cockpits for the core crew of four – a pilot, radio operator, bombardier and gunner.

With wood-framed wings, braced by a series of struts and cables and covered in fabric, and a metal tail section, the He 59 was capable of reaching speeds of 137 mph and had a range of 950 miles driven by two 660hp BMW engines. It was armed with two or three machine guns and could carry up to twenty 110lb bombs or a single torpedo. The first of two prototypes flew in September 1931 and, after further tests, the aircraft went into production in January 1932.

The He 59 quickly found a variety of uses as war approached, with later models kitted out for air-sea rescue operations. The Luftwaffe was years ahead of the RAF in launching a rescue service for pilots who crashed into the sea. The *Seenotdienst* was set up in early 1935, while the British equivalent did not come into being until 1941.

The *Seenotdienst* was founded by Lieutenant Konrad Goltz, a supply officer with the Luftwaffe based in the port of Kiel, and it was the first air-sea rescue service in the world. He co-ordinated his work with military units and civilian lifeboat societies as well as German marine organisations. The *Seenotdienst* was manned by both military and civilian personnel.

Later, with the growing probability of war with Great Britain, the organisation came under the auspices of the Luftwaffe and, in early 1939, the German air force carried out large-scale rescue exercises over water. New air bases were constructed along the coast to provide cover over large parts of the North Sea and the Baltic.

As the Battle of Britain approached its climax, the Germans placed highly visible yellow buoys in waters where their airmen were likely to be shot down. The floats held emergency supplies, including food, water, blankets and dry clothing for four men – and in some cases even bunks.

British airmen referred to these buoys as 'lobster pots' and both sides made use of them. Other creatures also found them hospitable; seals moved in on several occasions.

When the first multiple air-sea rescue operation of the war was launched on 19 December 1939, the Germans saved twenty British airmen who had been among the crews that flew twenty-two Wellington bombers on a mission to attack the port of Wilhelmshaven.

After running into heavy opposition from German fighters, more than half of the British force was shot down over the North Sea. German rescue boats based at Horkum, working with Heinkel 59s, then pulled several RAF crews from the icy waters.

The aircraft became the main workhorse for a service that correctly foresaw the danger to downed aircrew in the English Channel and elsewhere, and saved scores of men from drowning.

The He 59s of the type flown by Chudziak had their bomb-targeting equipment and machine guns removed. They featured glazed nose panels and carried six inflatable dinghies, an emergency medical kit, life belts, electrically heated sleeping bags, artificial respirator machines, special signalling equipment, grab ropes and a folding ladder that led from a hatch in the underside of the fuselage to help the crew rescue airmen in the water.

The first operational use of the He 59 had taken place in the Spanish Civil War, in which Chudziak also served, where the planes were deployed as bombers and on anti-shipping patrols. In the early months of the Second World War, He 59s were involved in action in northern Europe, when they were used to lay mines in the Thames estuary. One of their most famous deployments came during the German invasion of the Netherlands in May 1940, when up to twelve He 59s took off from north-west Germany, carrying 100 heavily trained infantry soldiers.

The aircraft made a quiet, gliding descent and landed on the River Meuse in the centre of Rotterdam, from where the troops made their way ashore using dinghies and promptly captured the Willems Bridge, one of the key crossing points over the river. The He 59s, meanwhile, took off again and made good their escape.

By 1943, all the remaining He 59s in service had been confined to training units. But what of the pilot on that late July night in 1940?

Erich Chudziak stares out from the official black and white portraits that appear in his military identification papers, and in the memorial book listing those lost in the Second World War who were members of the Evangelical Lutheran Church of St Nicolai in his native Westerland, on the island of Sylt.

There is an intensity – an alertness and earnestness – about him, dressed as he was in his immaculate service tunic. But we can only guess the true nature of this thirty-year-old Luftwaffe pilot, who was killed on his eighth day on the front line in the Battle of Britain.

He hailed from a beautiful strip of land thrust precariously into the edge of the North Sea, fringed by pristine sandy beaches and connected to the mainland by a causeway. The people of Sylt – an outpost on the north-west edge of Germany that, nowadays, is a popular holiday haunt of the rich – have always been a close-knit community.

Living in traditional thatched houses, the islanders battled over the centuries to keep the North Sea from washing their homes away and made their living as fishermen, as whaling crews and by cultivating oysters. The first tourists arrived there in the nineteenth century, enjoying a location favoured by retired sea captains.

Although listed as from the island, Chudziak is thought to have been born at Gelsenkirchen, near Dortmund. He had seven brothers and sisters and three half-sisters or brothers. His father was Adam Chudziak – the family name has Polish origins – who is described as a miner on Chudziak's identification papers. His mother was Anna Schlesier. Chudziak's papers indicate that he was awarded a campaign medal for service in Spain before his deployment on the English Channel coast.

He was married to Dorothea (née Schuler) who died in 2000, aged eighty-nine. The couple are remembered by a simple memorial plaque at the graveyard in Westerland. His entry in the church's memorial book reads:

'Erich Chudziak was a senior lieutenant in a rescue squadron. He was barely eight days at the front when he was shot down on the English Channel on 27 July 1940 with his machine, and died an aviator's death in faithful duty.'

When attempts were made to contact members of Chudziak's family through the church authorities on Sylt, they declined to help with this book. Johannes Sprenger, of the Sylter Archive in Westerland, reported that the family were anxious not to contribute to a 'glorification of the Nazis'.

Like most German organisations at the time, the *Seenotdienst* had been tainted by the Nazis. Much of its understanding of hypothermia, for example, was gained as a result of experiments carried out on prisoners at Dachau concentration camp. This involved submerging prisoners in extremely cold water and then warming them up in electrically heated sleeping bags. Up to 100 prisoners were said to have died during the experiments.

And the RAF was right. The Luftwaffe *was* using Heinkel 59s for monitoring convoys and reconnaissance, but the British had to disguise their sources. More than thirty years after the war had ended, it was revealed that the intelligence-gathering centre at Bletchley Park – the greatest secret of the war – had decoded Enigma traffic from Berlin directing the German air-sea rescue service to engage in military reconnaissance.

Erich Chudziak's Heinkel 59 had been a legitimate target after all.

*Russell 'Digger' Aitken, centre, scrounged a Walrus seaplane and saved
35 airmen who had been shot down over the Channel. Here he is pictured with
the pilots of No 3 Squadron later in the war*

4

Flight Lieutenant Russell Aitken
Supermarine Walrus Seaplane

1 August 1940

*They would take off to the rescue like a couple
of ducks swooping for bread over a pond.*

O NE OF THE shortcomings on the Allied side during the Battle
of Britain was the failure to provide sufficient rescue services
for pilots who crashed into the English Channel and the North
Sea. As we have seen, the Germans were doing their bit, even if
it was little more than a cover for reconnaissance work. So focused
was the British war effort on fighting and survival that military
planners did not give any priority to a properly resourced seaborne
and air-sea rescue service, despite the fact that much of the aerial
combat took place over water.

While the Germans deployed Heinkel 59 seaplanes from 1935
onwards, the Allied response was based solely on some Westland
Lysander spotter aircraft, lifeboats and launches. This was, however,
of little comfort to the RAF's fighter pilots in Hurricanes, Spitfires
and Defiants, who knew that their chances of survival in the water
at any time of year were not high, with many likely to die before
rescue, if it ever came.

During the last three weeks of July 1940, 220 Allied aircrew were
killed, or posted as missing, the majority of them over the sea. For
those who were picked up, it was more often by luck than judg-
ment. Among the lucky airmen in this respect was Pilot Officer
Eric Farnes, a gunner in a Boulton Paul Defiant with 141 Squadron.
He bailed out of his stricken aircraft and was picked up by a rescue

boat. 'I was bloody glad to feel that hook up my arse!' he recalled of being fished out of the water.

RAF fighter pilots were not supplied with a dinghy until 1941 and they took their chances over the Channel and the North Sea with only a hand-inflated lifejacket to preserve them. A pilot crashing or parachuting into the sea more than a mile offshore was thus likely to die of shock, exposure, drowning or the effects of injuries sustained in combat. Depending on the time of year, the sea temperature and conditions, pilots were likely to survive for as little as half an hour and certainly no more than four hours.

As a result, the RAF was losing scores of highly trained men – something that was bad for the prosecution of the battle and for morale. The losses prompted the setting up of a proper British air-and-sea rescue service after the Battle of Britain, but at the end of July in that critical summer of 1940 one man in the RAF decided to take the matter into his own hands.

In a little-known episode, a New Zealand-born pilot conceived the idea of employing amphibian aircraft, which can land and take off on ground and water, to retrieve pilots from the sea. Flight Lieutenant Russell 'Digger' Aitken, who was born to a farming family in Outram, Otago, on New Zealand's South Island, was stationed as an instructor with the Fleet Air Arm at Gosport in Hampshire.

He put his plan to his senior officers, who gave him the go-ahead. The former champion school sprinter managed to 'scrounge' a Supermarine Walrus – an ungainly looking but versatile seaplane with a rear-facing central propeller – from the Fleet Air Arm. He then began operating as a one-man air-sea rescue service.

According to the official history of New Zealanders in the RAF, Aitken would land his plane in the English Channel off the Isle of Wight and wait for the action to develop in the skies above him. He was not always alone.

'Sometimes a German Heinkel float-plane landed nearby on a similar mission and the two aircraft, watching each other suspiciously, would remain floating placidly on the sea until air battles started above,' the authors report.

In this way the two crews established a liaison of sorts and Aitken was quoted as saying that when planes were shot down, he and his

German counterparts would take off to the rescue 'like a couple of ducks swooping for bread over a pond'. Much of the detail of this curious relationship spanning the front line of the Battle of Britain has been lost, but it offers a remarkable example of people on both sides working together to save lives.

Aitken was engaged in this activity for several weeks, during which he picked up thirty-five British and German airmen. Other reports said that Aitken's flight – suggesting more than one Walrus may have been involved – picked up between sixty and seventy pilots. This is corroborated by other accounts indicating that Walrus aircraft from Royal Naval Air Station Ford in Sussex joined in the impromptu service being operated by Aitken. However, the bombing of Aitken's base at Gosport, and the airfield at Ford in late August, brought the effort to a premature end with the Walrus aircraft dispersed elsewhere.

Born in New Zealand on 15 September 1913 – a day now commemorated as Battle of Britain Day – Aitken attended Gore High School and Timaru Boys' High School. He was an outstanding runner who set records at 220 yards and 440 yards, and also ran for South Canterbury Amateur Athletic Club. When he left school, he briefly worked on the family farm, but left New Zealand in 1937 to join the RAF on a short service commission.

He had learnt to fly at his local aerodrome at Taieri, near Dunedin, according to a May 1941 report in the *Otago Daily Times*. The report is accompanied by a picture of Aitken taken 'somewhere in England' standing in full uniform alongside the Duke of Kent, who appears to be visiting his unit. Aitken had earlier fought over Dunkirk, flying one sortie after another for seven days with minimal sleep.

Seconded to the Fleet Air Arm in 1937, Aitken was appointed to the Royal Navy as an instructor on catapult aircraft. He served in HMS *Courageous*, a battle cruiser converted to an aircraft carrier and equipped with Fairey Swordfish biplanes. He then served in HMS *Furious*, another similarly converted battle cruiser, and finally on the aircraft carrier HMS *Ark Royal*.

During the Norwegian campaign in April 1940, Aitken was one of three pilots who ferried Hurricanes from *Ark Royal* to a base at Trondheim in central Norway. The New Zealand Press Association reported that he was lucky to survive an incident when the *Ark Royal* was bombed. As the huge carrier swerved in the wash from an explosion in the water close by, Aitken was swept overboard, but was quickly picked up. Perhaps it was this experience that convinced him that pilots must not be left to die in the sea.

In September 1940 he joined 3 Squadron, commanding the unit from December 1940 to May 1942 and completing two operational tours flying long-range Hurricanes. During that period, he was responsible for developmental work on long-range night intruders, which aimed to shoot down German bombers while they were landing on airfields in France after raids over England. In the course of this deployment, Aitken became the first pilot in a Hurricane single-engine night fighter armed with four cannon to shoot down a German bomber at night. He completed 1,000 hours on Hurricanes, nearly half of them on combat sorties.

He was appointed staff officer in charge of night operations with 11 Fighter Group in May 1942. During the 'Baedeker raids' in April and May of 1942, when the Luftwaffe targeted cities of cultural and historical value such as Exeter, Bath, York and Canterbury, Aitken was responsible for co-ordinating the RAF's defence.

That September, at the age of twenty-nine, he was appointed head of the RAF station at Hawkinge in Kent, becoming the youngest station commander in Fighter Command. After that he commanded the RAF station at Bradwell Bay in Essex.

He was awarded the Air Force Cross in 1943 for his developmental work on night fighters and the OBE in 1944 as an acting wing commander. He was mentioned in dispatches three times, first for his air-sea rescue flights, then for helping to develop the single-engine night fighter, and finally for his response to the Baedeker raids.

Aitken finished his career as a group captain and was appointed CBE. He left the RAF in 1957. His wife, Rhoda, was three years older than him and died in 1984. After returning to New Zealand, Aitken served as a justice of the peace. He died in 1989, aged seventy-six, and is buried in St Albans Anglican Cemetery in Porirua, Wellington. His gravestone records that he was 'fondly known and dearly loved as "Digger"'.

Given its unwieldy appearance, it is hard to believe that the Supermarine Walrus was designed by R.J. Mitchell, the man who also designed the Supermarine Spitfire. First flown in 1933, it was an amphibious biplane devised to be catapult-launched from battle cruisers for use in a spotter or reconnaissance role. It was conceived in response to an order in 1929 from the Royal Australian Air Force (RAAF) and was originally called the Seagull V. The RAAF took delivery of twenty-four planes in 1935, with the first of twelve planes ordered by the RAF flying the following year. In all, 740 Walruses were built to three specifications between 1936 and 1944.

The distinctive features of the aircraft were its all-metal main fuselage, its large, almost top-heavy slightly swept back fabric-covered wings and its single engine, which was mounted facing backwards under the upper wing. The planes were fitted with two machine guns and could carry bombs or depth charges if required. Once catapult-launched from a ship, the planes would return after their missions to land alongside and be lifted by crane back into their cradle. There was a crew of up to four in the Walrus, a pilot, sometimes a co-pilot, a navigator and a radio operator.

A tricky aircraft to fly, the Walrus was known by its aircrews variously as the 'Shagbat' or 'Steam-pigeon' because of the steam created when water sprayed on to its Pegasus engine. Land-based take-offs and landings were fairly straightforward, but such manoeuvres could be challenging in even moderate sea conditions offshore.

'The old girl had to be dropped into a landing right on top of the swell,' recalled one air-sea rescue pilot Flight Lieutenant Nick Berryman. 'If the pilot missed, and hit the following trough, the next swell could hurl the aircraft back into the air, but with no flying speed, and in a deep stall; the bigger the wave top, the higher one was hurled, and the resulting landing was,' said Berryman, 'both wet and interesting. The Walrus, however, was a tough old bird, and took a lot of punishment.' Generally, he said, landings were made without too much damage.

Taking off in rough seas required quick reactions from the pilot, as the plane bounced and flew in turn as it tried to escape the waves for the air. When rescuing downed pilots, Walrus aircrews would always land and worry about taking off and getting home afterwards, even if that meant having to be towed for hours to the nearest harbour if sea conditions made it impossible to get airborne again.

The Walrus was a tough old bird, often catapulted from ships; rescuing a pilot in 1941

Ungainly, it might have been, but the Walrus saved the lives of hundreds of aircrew. There are believed to be only four such planes still in existence: one at the Royal Air Force Museum in London; another at the Fleet Air Arm Museum at Yeovilton in Somerset; and a third at the Royal Australian Air Force Museum in Victoria. The fourth is in private hands in the UK.

Once the absence of adequate resources for rescuing pilots in the sea became clear, the Royal Navy and RAF moved quickly to improve and co-ordinate the emergency response. By the end of August 1940, the framework of a sea-rescue organisation had been agreed, with all rescue vessels coming under the operational control of local naval authorities. The RAF was responsible for air searches and informing the naval authorities.

In the face of continued losses at sea, the organisation was radically reformed and expanded in December 1940 and by January 1941 a director of Sea Rescue Services was appointed and based at HQ Coastal Command at Northwood in Middlesex. In the first four months after the appointment of the director, the proportion of rescues increased from 20 per cent to 35 per cent of downed aircrews.

By the summer of 1941, even greater resources were channelled into the rescue effort as dedicated squadrons were deployed, the number of RAF and Royal Navy fast launches was increased, and the development of survival aids led to more lives being saved.

*A portrait of Edward Lart in full dress uniform. Renowned for his courage,
Lart was regarded as a demanding and daring commander, who had been
a precocious child taught to show no fear*

5

Wing Commander Edward Collis
de Virac Lart
Bristol Blenheim Light Bomber

13 August 1940

With a sense of growing invincibility,
Lart reached targets that were beyond other crews.

A S THE PILOT of a bomber leading what became known as the
'doomed squadron', Wing Commander Edward Lart appeared
to have a death wish. While undoubtedly courageous, he was also
eccentric and reckless, a man with no known personal relationships,
who pressed home an attack on a German aerodrome in Denmark
in defiance of his orders.

The consequences of Lart's actions were tragic – the loss of the
entire attacking force of eleven Blenheim bombers from 82 Squadron.
Perhaps unsurprisingly, historians have not been kind to Lart. In
his influential book, *Bomber Command*, Max Hastings describes him
as 'a chilly, ruthless officer, who feared nothing himself and had no
sympathy for others who obviously did.'

The date of Lart's mission was a momentous one: 13 August
1940 – dubbed *Adlertag* or 'Eagle Day' by the Germans – which
had been earmarked by Goering, the head of the Luftwaffe, as the
start of its main assault on RAF bases in southern England.

At thirty-eight, Lart was an experienced pilot, a British veteran
of the RAF who had led the Norfolk-based Blenheims for two
months. A force of twelve aircraft under his command took off
from Watton aerodrome and its satellite field at Bodney at about
8.30 a.m. At their briefing the crews – three men in each aircraft

– were told that the mission would be aborted if there was less than five-tenths cloud. The sky was clear.

Their target was an aerodrome – Fliegerhorst Aalborg West – in northern Denmark, where the Germans were building up a fleet of Junkers 52 transport planes. Until recently, the base had been little more than a grass field, but it had proved its worth during the Norway campaign and it was being upgraded by the occupiers using slave labour. According to intelligence reports, it was being prepared as a transport hub for the invasion of Britain.

Already experienced in this kind of mission, Lart was known for being an ambitious, demanding and daring commander. He had taken part in several missions in July before the Battle of Britain started and later as the conflict developed.

On 7 July, he flew 300 miles into enemy territory, alone and in daylight, to attack Eschwege airfield in central Germany, south-east of Kassel; on 13 July, he found an enemy oil refinery and bombed it from 1,000ft; three days later, he flew so low in thick mist against the German fighter station at St Inglevert in the Pas de Calais that he could not drop his 250lb bombs for fear of blowing himself out of the sky. Even the smaller 40lb bombs caused some damage to his own machine.

When eight out of ten crews turned back on 18 July, Lart pressed on to attack invasion barges; and on 28 July, his was the only one of seven crews to bomb an airfield at Leeuwarden in the Netherlands. His Blenheim was attacked by four German fighters on the return flight, but he eluded the cannons of the Messerschmitt Bf 109s and his gunner, Sergeant Gus Beeby, claimed one 'probably shot down'. When he landed, Lart's damaged Blenheim was rendered unflyable; his crew survived. Three days later he was recommended for the Distinguished Service Order by Air Commodore James Robb.

A similar pattern continued into August. Perhaps with a sense of growing invincibility, Lart reached targets that were beyond other crews.

On 6 August, he led the squadron on a low-level raid over Boulogne in northern France. According to the squadron's Operational Record Book: 'Of these 14 aircraft which set off to attack enemy aerodromes, 13 came back owing to lack of cloud cover.' The one aircraft that did not turn back was Lart's, which suffered superficial damage from its own bombs.

According to Hastings, who does not name Lart in his book, the wing commander [Lart] summoned all the crews to gaze at the damage. "'*That* is the way I expect crews to bomb, and *that* is the height at which I expect them to attack," he announced furiously.'

Hastings added: 'The squadron shrugged its shoulders. Even when crews were being lost faster than they could unpack, they did not shrink from doing the job. But they shared no enthusiasm for a man who was obviously indifferent to his own survival.'

The Blenheims of 82 Squadron, part of 2 Group, had already suffered disproportionately, flying aircraft that were simply inadequate for daylight operations against German land forces, Luftwaffe bases and enemy shipping. Over a period of five years, the Blenheim, one of the first aircraft to be built with an all-metal stressed skin, had been transformed from one of the most formidable military machines to one of the most vulnerable. It had been commissioned as an executive plane by the newspaper magnate Lord Rothermere and was flown for the first time on 12 April 1935.

Afterwards Rothermere ordered two Hamilton variable-pitch propellers from America to replace the aircraft's wooden blades, increasing the aircraft's speed from 260 mph to just over 300 mph – 80 mph faster than any fighter in the RAF and 20 mph faster than any American aircraft. A sleek, majestic machine, the Bristol Blenheim was 42ft long, with a wingspan of 57ft and two Mercury radial engines.

In August 1935, on behalf of his flagship newspaper, the *Daily Mail*, Rothermere formally presented the prototype to the RAF as 'a peace gift'. It would later have a bomb load of just over 1,000lb.

By 1939 the Blenheim light bomber, weighed down by armaments, was much slower than the Luftwaffe's fighters and incapable of withstanding punishment in a determined attack. It had a single Browning machine gun in the port wing, another in a rear-firing blister and two in an upper turret. Its only chance of survival during daylight raids was to hide in the clouds.

On 17 May, eleven out of twelve Blenheims from 82 Squadron had been destroyed while attacking a German armoured column at Gembloux in central Belgium and the squadron suffered further losses throughout the summer. Few aircraft ever returned from raids undamaged. The same probably applied to the men inside the aircraft, who occasionally cracked, but more often went back into combat.

Lart was given the fateful order for the attack on Aalborg on the afternoon of 12 August and prepared his men for the mission by sending them off for a night on the town in Norwich, although they were instructed not to be back late.

The next morning, the crews were divided into two groups of six aircraft: Lart led A flight from Watton, while Squadron Leader 'Rusty' Wardell led B flight from Bodney. They would be operating at the limit of the Blenheim's range and were told that they should not try to return to base. Instead, they should land wherever possible in Scotland or northern England.

From the outset, problems delayed the mission. In his haste to board an aircraft, one airman accidentally released his parachute and had to fetch a replacement. Then another crew, led by Don McFarlane, were called back even as they were warming up their engines; a mechanic who had been opening the post came running out to inform them that they had been stood down from operations and transferred to instructing duties. A standby crew took their place.

While all this was going on, another airman, Bill Magrath, developed his usual practice of quietly eating his chocolate ration before take-off in case he was shot down. He hated the idea of chocolate being wasted.

As Lart's force headed across the North Sea, more problems developed. Sergeant Norman Baron, flying one of the Blenheims in B flight, noticed that his gauges showed that he was low on fuel and turned back. It was not the first time he had aborted a mission, and some of his colleagues were growing suspicious. After landing, Baron was placed under arrest.

The remaining eleven Blenheims continued their flight with orders to attack from an altitude of 20,000ft, which made it virtually impossible to strike their target with any accuracy. Crossing the North Sea in thick cloud at 5,000ft, the aircraft climbed to 8,000ft as they approached the Danish coast.

At that moment, the all-important cloud cover disappeared. Lart's orders had been clear in this event: he should abort the mission. Instead, true to character, he pressed on at relatively low altitude.

Other factors also started to count against the men of 82 Squadron. Buffeted by strong winds, the eleven Blenheims had flown too far south. Some navigators in the formation realised the error and flashed their Aldis lamps, which were their only means of communication because of radio silence. Yet Beeby, the gunner in Lart's Blenheim, failed to see their signals.

The navigational error also alerted the Luftwaffe to the presence of the British force, which was registered by a German air observation post at Sondervig on the Danish coast. Blame for this rested with the inexperienced navigator leading the mission in Lart's aircraft. He was Pilot Officer Maurice Gillingham, aged twenty-two, a newcomer who generated resentment among the other crews, who suspected snobbery. Lart had chosen a fellow officer irrespective of his abilities, rather than a proven navigator from a different background.

The doomed British squadron now faced a run across Denmark in bright sunshine. As they headed north-east towards Aalborg, the Germans plotted their destruction.

While Lart descended to 3,000ft followed by the rest of A Flight, with B Flight not far behind, the first Bf 109s attacked the formation twenty miles from Aalborg. Several Blenheims jettisoned their bombs in an effort to survive. Unknown to Lart, nine Bf 109s had landed at Aalborg from Stavanger in Norway. As soon as the air-raid warning sounded, these fighters took off again. German anti-aircraft batteries were also ready for 82 Squadron's arrival. There was a savage, one-sided encounter.

Some of the British bombs hit their target, but little damage was inflicted. On the ground, one Danish worker was killed, and two more died later from their wounds. There were no German casualties.

In the air it was a different story. Over the next few minutes, the remaining Blenheims were destroyed by the German defences. Lart's aircraft was among the last to be brought down, hitting the ground about twenty-five miles beyond Aalborg and in sight of the coast. Lart, Gillingham and Beeby were all killed. Their bodies were checked by a Dr Ludvig Christensen from Brovost

Hospital later in the day. Only Gillingham could be identified at the time.

Of the thirty-six aircrew who set out on the mission, three turned back early, thirteen were taken prisoner, many of them with appalling injuries, and twenty were killed.

Baron was acquitted at a court martial of 'dereliction of duty and cowardice in the face of the enemy'. Nearly a year later, on 8 July 1941, his courage was recognised with a Distinguished Flying Medal. Two weeks after that, he was shot down and killed.

Magrath, who had long since finished his chocolate rations, was one of those taken prisoner. He was found by a Danish fishing vessel floating in the sea after his Blenheim was forced down by fighters, but he had a smashed leg and hip, a broken shoulder and was blind in one eye. Remarkably, Magrath later escaped from a camp in Rouen, northern France, and crossed the Pyrenees. He reached England in March 1942, the first witness to the carnage over Aalborg to return home. He was awarded the Military Medal.

The squadron's official Operations Record Book records: '4 sections set out to bomb Aalborg airport. Eleven aircraft missing. Weather fair or fine, becoming cloudy. Visibility 4–6 miles. Wind westerly, light.'

On the ground at Watton, McFarlane, who had been pulled off the mission at the last minute, was listening to a radio report by Lord Haw-Haw, the English voice of Nazi Germany, who said: 'This morning eleven aircraft of the Blenheim type approached Aalborg in Denmark. Six were shot down by anti-aircraft fire and five by fighters.'

According to Hastings, McFarlane and his crew burst into noisy laughter at this blatant propaganda. 'It was only towards tea, when the empty airfield still lay in silence, that the terrible reality sank home to them . . . For once, Lord Haw-Haw reported the literal truth.'

Adlertag, the launch of the Luftwaffe's main attacks on the RAF in the south of England, did not go to plan either. The British radar stations identified big German formations from as early as 5 a.m., with the Luftwaffe flying 1,485 sorties during the course of the day, the largest number so far.

While they bombed several airfields, their targets were not always the vital bases belonging to Fighter Command. The Coastal Command stations at Eastchurch and Detling were both hit, with many casualties. In a day of intense aerial combat: the Luftwaffe is believed to have lost thirty-nine aircraft, with sixty-six airmen killed; and the RAF fifteen fighters, with four pilots killed.

Both sides claimed far more kills than they achieved. German intelligence believed that more than 100 British aircraft had been shot down, raising expectations that Fighter Command was on the verge of collapse. As Air Chief Marshal Sir Hugh Dowding is reported to have told Archibald Sinclair, the Secretary of State for Air: 'If the Germans' figures were accurate, they would be in London in a week, otherwise they would not.'

At the time, Lart's nephew John was living with his grandparents. In an interview for this book, he looked back with some emotion on the day when a messenger arrived carrying the news that his uncle was missing. 'It's been a great shame to me, because I didn't understand the significance of the telegraph boy,' he said. 'So I sniggered.'

He recalled how his grandfather had gone out to meet the messenger after spotting the boy walking up the path. 'He came back and said to his wife, "Amy, come with me." They were very upset.'

Many years later, Hastings questioned why the Blenheims were sent out on a mission that was almost certainly suicidal, with little prospect of causing significant damage to the German aerodrome. 'The Aalborg operation', he wrote, 'was a disaster reflecting almost Crimean stupidity on the part of those at Bomber Command and Group who ordered it.'

The man who led the mission, Edward Collis de Virac Lart, was the son of Charles Edmund Lart and his wife, Amy. Charles was a historian who believed that he was descended from a Huguenot family and liked to give his children romantic names from mythical French ancestors. They lived at Knapp Cottage in Charmouth, Dorset.

Edward, who was born on 27 March 1902, was the third of five children. An elder brother, Edmund, known as Ted, lost a leg while serving with the Dorsetshire Regiment in the Great War, but lived into his eighties, stomping around shooting grouse in Scotland. An elder sister, Kathleen, known as Jo, spoke fluent German. After the war she lived in Bonn and Berlin and in 1945 was the first of the family to visit Edward's grave. He also had a younger sister, Judith.

His younger brother, John, became a doctor and served in the Royal Army Medical Corps; he was killed on 4 January 1944, on the approaches to Monte Cassino in Italy. He is buried at the Cassino War Cemetery.

According to John Lart Jr, it was considered 'very important' as they were growing up 'not to show fear'. The family legend has it that Edward and his siblings enjoyed something of a wild childhood similar to that in *The Railway Children*, the book by Edith Nesbitt.

In 1913, the family moved to a house in Lyme Regis called Navarah, which was named after the town in the Basque country. Edward was educated at Weymouth College, which was then a minor public school.

In a letter written to his mother, which is reproduced in Gordon Thorburn's book, *The Squadron That Died Twice*, the young Lart comes across as a confident, opinionated boy:

Dear Mother,
I got that shirt. Whatever made you address it to the Junior School. If you address things to Weymouth College it will get there allright. The work in 4B is disgusting stuff which John could easily do. I haven't had half such a bad time as expected. Will you write and tell me if I can join the OTC. We had shooting practice the other day. There's an awful piano to practice on but Mrs Conway lets me do it on hers. Mr Thom is an ass; he wanted to put me on to some silly sonata or other that I learned years ago. If you wrote and told him sharply that I must do some things (I'll send you the no's of the pages of some nice ones), he'd soon shut up. Please address letters E Lart.
   Much love from
   Edward

He later took up a place at St Catharine's College, Cambridge, graduating in mathematics and physics, before going to RAF Cranwell. On 15 September 1924, he was granted a permanent commission as a pilot officer. According to RAF records, he collided with another aircraft while serving with 5 Flying Training School, but was not injured.

By 1925 Lart was in India, serving with a bomber squadron based at Kohat in the north of what is now Pakistan. While there he flew the Airco DH9A, a First World War design that had been adapted in the 1920s for general duties.

He was involved in the forced landing of a Russian aircraft in 1928, which is mentioned in a memorandum from HQ Royal Air Force India. A year later, his was believed to have been among the first aircraft to fly through the Khyber Pass when the RAF evacuated about 600 civilians from Kabul.

Lart qualified as an interpreter and in 1931 was mentioned in dispatches for active service on the North West Frontier. His commanding officer, Group Captain Roger Neville, MC, later wrote to Lart's younger sister, Judith, about their time serving the British Empire in India. 'Not only did he show himself to be an able and gallant officer; he was a charming friend to my family; quiet and unassuming in character; and extremely popular with all the right sort of people.'

Lart also kept diaries, now in the possession of his nephew, which record the shooting of tigers and the cost of keeping 'coolies' and servants.

Returning to Britain in 1931, he joined a fighter squadron, but by 1937 he had been promoted to squadron leader and given command of one of the newly formed bomber squadrons.

He had no family of his own. Indeed, the only one of the five Lart siblings to have children was John, who worked as a medical missionary in Iran before the war. John Jr was born in November 1933. Edward was one of his godfathers and is believed to have been present at his christening in early 1934. John Jr recalled only one visit by his godfather.

'He drove us up from Plymouth to Sidmouth in my father's little Austin 7,' he said. 'I was sitting behind Edward. I remember he had his tongue stuck in his cheek, which I found amusing at the age of five or so.' They visited the seaside at Ladram Bay, where there is a notable rock stack. 'I remember my father and Edward climbing this and bombing or diving off it,' he recalled. 'I was very impressed by their athleticism.'

In his letter to Lart's sister Judith, Neville recalled that her brother, then in Iraq, had agitated at the start of the war for a posting to an operational squadron in Britain. 'I advised him to wait his turn and told him it would come, I thought, with Italy's entrance to the war.'

Neville was right. Soon enough Lart was back in Britain, where he quickly learnt to fly Blenheims and took part in a number of operations before being given command of 82 Squadron in June 1940. He succeeded Paddy Brandon, the 5th Earl of Brandon, a charismatic aristocrat and popular commander, who had been promoted to group captain. The two men could not have sat in starker contrast: the warmth of Brandon ranged against the apparent coldness of Lart. He revealed very little about his past, which led to wild and uninformed speculation.

Lart's sister-in-law, Ted's wife Molly, recalled him as being a mysterious, romantic figure, who would turn up unannounced wearing an opera cape and whisk them off to the theatre. Yet any information about his personal life died with him. His nephew, John Jr, insisted that the family had no knowledge of any personal relationships of a romantic nature, but he added: 'I really couldn't be sure.'

Three days after the raid on Aalborg, Lart and the nineteen other RAF crewmen who died were buried by the Germans, who considered them to have acted with the utmost gallantry. They received full military honours, including a 36-rifle salute.

Today their graves are among thirty in Vadum cemetery, about four miles north of Aalborg, in a corner of a churchyard that is maintained by the Commonwealth War Graves Commission. They are buried alongside four men from 102 Squadron, who were killed in a Whitley bomber on 26 April 1940; and six from 10 Squadron, who were killed when their Halifax bomber was destroyed on 15 October 1944.

Lart and his brother John are also remembered on the war memorial in the centre of the village of Newton Poppleford, in Devon. Another memorial is mounted on the south wall in the Church of St Gregory the Great at Harpford, near his parents' home.

On 4 June 1941, a notice appeared in *The Times*, declaring: 'Wing

*Blenheims of No 42
Squadron at Watton*

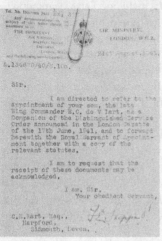

*The burial of British crews in
Denmark, where they were
honoured by the Germans;
and the letter confirming
Lart's DSO*

Commander Edward Collis de Virac Lart, previously reported missing, now officially presumed killed in action.' It gave no account of the circumstances of his death. More than a year later, the same newspaper published a tribute by Neville, which described Lart's 'zest for action' and his impatience to have 'a crack at Hitler'.

Neville also responded to a request from Lart's mother for memories of her son. In a letter dated 8 February 1942, Neville wrote:

I am sure that no one outside his own family could miss him more than we do. We spent some memorable holidays together; and my son – who is shortly entering the RAF himself – has held Edward in the highest esteem as a playmate and companion since they first combined to flout nursery authority fourteen years ago in Kohat.

An 'In Memoriam' notice, which appeared in *The Times* on 13 August 1942, mentioned that Lart had been killed in action on that date two years earlier. In March 1946, Wing Commander E.F. Pippett wrote to Neville with a summary of the information that had been gathered about the raid, describing it with some understatement as 'one of our more disorganised efforts'.

On 13 August 2013, seventy-three years after the fateful Aalborg mission, two memorial stones were unveiled at the Tranum Dune Plantation, where two of the aircraft, including Lart's, came down. The initiative for the memorial came from a local walking group, who heard the story of the raid while exploring the woods. 'We were just looking,' recalled Lillian Carstensen, one of their number. 'There was nothing to see . . . we found that a bit sad.'

During the unveiling, the Baby Blue display team of the Royal Danish Airforce made a flypast. John Lart Jr was present with his wife, Katherine, and three of their four children.

A retired gynaecologist and consultant obstetrician, John Jr is a measured and thoughtful man. '[Edward] was reckoned in the family to be incredibly brave,' John Jr said. 'But I have learnt since that he was considered foolhardy. In fact, although he was cited for a DSO before he died, it wasn't confirmed until a whole year later, because the top brass in the RAF didn't think he should be memorialised.'

The award of the DSO, one of the highest for gallantry, was finally made on 17 June 1941, in recognition of Lart's attack on the German airfield at Leeuwarden in the Netherlands on 28 July 1940, during the Battle of Britain.

It read: 'By his courage, devotion to duty and skill as a pilot he has set an inspiring example which has more than maintained the excellent esprit de corps of all ranks under his command.'

The Swiss pilot Walter Rubensdorffer standing in front of his Mercedes staff car in August 1940. He commanded a specialist unit known as 'Test Wing 210' that attacked Britain's radar stations

6

Flight Lieutenant Walter Rubensdorffer
Messerschmitt Bf 110 Jabo Fighter-Bomber

15 August 1940

There was something almost messianic about him –
and he led from the front.

L IKE MANY OF the young men fighting and dying in the skies
over England in the summer of 1940, Walter Rubensdorffer
was fanatical about flying. He had even stated in his will that, when
he died, his ashes were to be scattered from an aeroplane.

Unlike Goering and many of the senior German generals,
Rubensdorffer also had ideas about how to prosecute a war in the
air and his vision influenced the course of the Battle of Britain. He
was the commander of an elite Luftwaffe unit known as 'Test Wing
210'. Members of the unit had a distinct emblem painted on either
side of the nose cone of their aircraft: a red map of Britain within
a yellow gunsight.

On the morning of Monday, 12 August, Rubensdorffer refrained
from engaging in any kind of casual conversation with his pilots.
According to *The Luftwaffe War Diaries*, by Cajus Bekker, the Swiss
pilot was preoccupied. He had just been given the most important
mission of the war to date: the destruction of the radio direction
finding (RDF) stations – now known as radar – whose lattice masts
stood like dystopian figures from an H.G. Wells story along the
southern and eastern coastlines of England.

It was General Wolfgang Martini, the Luftwaffe's chief signals
officer, who had begun to understand the vital role of the radar
system, with its masts and transmission huts. He understood the
way in which the British had organised their RDF stations to detect

German aircraft above the coast of France, thus removing the element of surprise on which the Luftwaffe's squadrons depended for success.

The RDF stations sat at the heart of a system built by Air Chief Marshal Sir Hugh Dowding during the late 1930s to defend Britain from air attack. Radar allowed Fighter Command to plan ahead with the first 'sightings' appearing on cathode-ray tubes in receiver huts tracking radio signals picked up by the masts.

While General Martini understood this, he had difficulty convincing others. According to Edward Fennessy, a radar expert with the Air Ministry in London, Martini 'had to argue very forcibly with Goering to allow the Luftwaffe to attack the RDF stations'. Goering's attitude, said Fennessy, was that the Luftwaffe was an offensive air force and it was not going to bother with any new-fangled defensive devices. He wanted to get on with the air war. However, Martini persuaded him to allow some attacks.

On 12 August, visibility was excellent as Rubensdorffer made his way towards the English coast at the controls of his Messerschmitt 110 fighter-bomber. According to Bekker, he called the commander of one of the squadrons accompanying him. 'Proceed on special mission,' he said. 'Good hunting.'

Led by First Lieutenant Otto Hintze, eight Messerschmitt Bf 109 fighter-bombers headed for Dover, while Rubensdorffer flew inland to lead an attack on the radar station at the Kent village of Dunkirk, near Canterbury. Two other sections flew along the English coast, heading south-west. Pevensey was the first station to be targeted and the bombing was extraordinarily accurate. One building took a direct hit and the main power cable was severed. Pevensey ceased transmitting.

Further east, the radar station at Rye was hit by ten bombs, according to German combat reports. At Dunkirk, one bomb virtually destroyed the building housing the transmitter, and at Dover, Hintze's Bf 109s damaged two radar masts. On the Isle of Wight, another radar station at Ventnor was virtually destroyed by 150 German aircraft, including Stuka dive bombers.

With four of the five radar stations out of action, and with surprise now on their side as a result, Rubensdorffer's fighter-bombers struck again in the early afternoon. This time their target was the RAF fighter base at Manston on the Kent coast. They arrived just as the Spitfires of 65 Squadron were trying to take off and caused havoc. Manston disappeared under a cloud of smoke. It was a similar story when the unit returned again that evening to attack RAF Hawkinge.

The day was a memorable one for the commander of Test Wing 210. Rubensdorffer exuded confidence, which was evident in the air and on the ground and can be seen in a black and white photograph taken of him in August 1940.

Dressed in his Luftwaffe uniform, Rubensdorffer stands with his arms loosely by his side, a heavily drawn cigarette in his left hand, his right knee slightly bent, one foot on the running board of a Mercedes staff car. He smiles broadly at the photographer and looks like a man at ease with himself, which is not surprising.

A rising star of the Luftwaffe, he was responsible for the development of what is sometimes referred to by modern video-gamers engaged in virtual warfare as the 'Rubensdorffer Doctrine': precision raids by small numbers of fighter-bombers, which he believed could do more damage than massed ranks of aircraft.

Even today Rubensdorffer can be found on websites that promote paintings and models of his aircraft, the Me 110D fighter-bomber known in German as a 'jabo'; and his exploits have been recounted in many languages, including Chinese, Dutch and Spanish.

Rubensdorffer was born on 1 August 1910 in the German-speaking city of Basel, on the banks of the Rhine, close to where the borders of Switzerland, Germany and France meet. Little appears to have been recorded about his upbringing, or his political views, and reports that he was a fanatical Nazi drawn to Hitler must be treated with care. His career with the German military started under the Weimar Republic, then a democratic regime, when he was seventeen.

According to the official career summaries of Luftwaffe officers, Rubensdorffer started flying with the German Air Transport School in April 1928. He received his advanced flying certificate in January 1932. Later that year, several months before Hitler was appointed as Chancellor, Rubensdorffer undertook further training at the German air combat school at Lipetsk in Russia, which had been set up in 1925 under a secret agreement between the two countries.

Rubensdorffer joined the German infantry in 1934, just as the Nazis were starting to expand the armed forces. Yet only a few months later, he was transferred to a unit set up under the auspices of the German Air Sports Association as part of a covert air force.

As Germany pushed ahead with rearmament and revealed the existence of its new military forces in 1935, Rubensdorffer was among the first pilots to join the new air force – the Luftwaffe. He was attached to a fighter wing and undertook further advanced training, including an instrument flying course at Celle in Lower Saxony.

His progress was rapid. By 1936 he had been given command of a squadron and a year later, at the age of twenty-six, he was promoted to *hauptmann*, the youngest pilot in the Luftwaffe to attain such a rank – the equivalent of a flight lieutenant in the RAF or a captain in the US Air Force.

In 1937, along with many of the pilots who would distinguish themselves during the Battle of Britain, Rubensdorffer joined the German Condor Legion and gained combat experience fighting on the side of Franco's nationalists in the Spanish Civil War. He is said to have become an expert in ground-attack missions, flying the Heinkel 51 biplane, and he was also credited with shooting down one republican aircraft.

He was later sent on a ground-attack course at Tutow in north-eastern Germany, one of the largest pilot training schools in the country. He was given command of a squadron of Stuka dive bombers, and then sent to the aviation ministry in Berlin, where he worked on the tactics of ground-attack aircraft. Here Rubensdorffer was in a position to influence strategy.

He was appointed commander of Test Wing 210 on 1 July 1940, only ten days before the start of the Battle of Britain. The unit was formed at the Koln-Ostheim aerodrome on the edge of the Ruhr with three existing Luftwaffe squadrons. Their task: to evaluate experimental weapons and assess new tactics.

The new wing was intended to be equipped with Me 210s, which were designed for attacking targets on the ground, but that aircraft was plagued by technical faults and, in the end, did not enter service until 1943. Instead, Rubensdorffer was provided with two squadrons of the latest twin-engine Me 110 fighters – the only aircraft in the Luftwaffe to be equipped with a huge 30mm cannon – and one squadron of Bf 109s.

Designed by Willy Messerschmitt as a heavy fighter, the Me 110 first flew in 1936 and was armed with powerful weaponry: two forward-firing 20mm cannons and four machine guns, as well as a rear gun in the cockpit. It could also carry two 1,000lb bombs. Under Rubensdorffer, the men of Test Wing 210 worked hard and appeared to make up for any weaknesses in their flying machines through their own skills as pilots.

Rubensdorffer is described as a man with an infectious sense of humour, but also as a resolute leader, who insisted that his crews followed his orders and implemented the tactics he was trying to develop. Indeed, there was something almost messianic about him – and he led from the front.

Test Wing 210 left Cologne on 10 July and headed for Denain in north-eastern France, close to the Belgian border, where it was part of Air Fleet 2 under the command of General Field Marshal Albert Kesselring. The airmen had quarters on the airfield or in the houses of French families who had fled the town. They would use St Omer–Arques and Calais–Marck, which were nearer the coast, as staging posts for their missions against targets in England.

During the first phase of the Battle of Britain, Test Wing 210 struck hard against British shipping. According to Bekker: 'It proved what the Luftwaffe chiefs hoped: that fighters too could carry bombs to a target – and attack and hit it.'

Rubensdorffer's men flew their first mission of the battle on 13 July, against two convoys at the mouth of the Thames. By the end of July, the unit claimed to have sunk 89,000 tons of shipping, including four British warships, and shot down three enemy aircraft. The pilots then withdrew for rest and further training.

On 11 August, they destroyed barrage balloons protecting the port of Dover and attacked a coastal convoy codenamed 'Booty'. At 1 p.m. about twenty-four aircraft dived on the shipping through anti-aircraft fire. Two large ships were severely damaged.

After breaking away, the unit was followed by Spitfires from 74 Squadron. Rubensdorffer immediately formed a defensive circle with his Me 110s while the Bf 109s attacked the Spitfires. Two Me

A radar station with its lattice mast, and the twin-engine Jabos of 'Test Wing 210' later in the war

110s were shot down, with the crews lost at sea, but three Spitfires were also destroyed in the encounter.

After the successful raids on the Kent RDF stations, Rubensdorffer might have been expected to hit other targets in the radar chain, but Goering was not convinced. All the radar stations attacked by Test Wing 210 on 12 August were repaired overnight and they were once again relaying information about the positions of German aircraft the next day.

Ernest Clark, a wireless operator working on radar at the time, said: 'It's very difficult to do damage to an RDF site. The lattice masts can't be seen from the air and they were so designed that they could stand up on any two of their gimbals. And the blast used to go through them.'

The radar station at Ventnor on the Isle of Wight was seriously damaged, however, and was out of action for nearly two weeks, but the British transmitted dummy radio signals from the site, giving the Germans the impression that it was still operational.

Goering fell for the ruse. In what was probably one of the most far-reaching and unwise decisions of the battle, he halted the attacks on the RDF stations, saying: 'It is doubtful whether there is any point in continuing the attacks on radar sites, in view of the fact that not one of those attacked so far has been put out of action.' Instead, he ordered the Luftwaffe to concentrate on the RAF's fighter airfields.

On 14 August, heavy cloud over the Channel restricted German operations, but Rubensdorffer's men were ordered to launch another mission against Manston.

At 12.05 p.m., the Me 110s – sixteen according to German combat reports, nine according to British records – swept in under low cloud, once again surprising the defenders, and successfully bombed four hangars, which were set ablaze. The airfield's gunners hit two of the German aircraft. High above the clouds, the Spitfires of 65 Squadron and the Hurricanes of 151 Squadron saw nothing of the attack.

The next day Colonel Paul Deichman, the chief of staff of the second air corps, issued orders for what would turn out to be the heaviest assault on Britain during the Battle of Britain: the Luftwaffe flew more than 2,000 sorties in eight hours.

SIMON PEARSON AND ED GORMAN

Rubensdorffer was in the air at about 1 p.m. While more than 100 German aircraft headed for Kent, the Me 110s of Test Wing 210 used the bigger raid as cover and flew unopposed towards the RAF base at Martlesham Heath in Suffolk. In a raid that lasted little more than half an hour, Rubensdorffer's men destroyed hangars and workshops, stores and communications facilities. The runway was left pockmarked with craters.

As well as Martlesham Heath, the Luftwaffe had already badly damaged the RAF bases at Hawkinge and Lympne in Kent, which would be out of action for several days, and targeted airfields in Scotland and the north of England.

Later that afternoon, Test Wing 210, by now among the most revered units in the Luftwaffe, was given the task of attacking the fighter base at Kenley, one of the key sector stations just south of London. Other units were scheduled to bomb Biggin Hill.

At 7.35 p.m., with the sun low in the sky and a haze beginning to obscure the ground, Rubensdorffer crossed the English coast at Dungeness. His fighter escort was meant to be close behind, but never made contact. In an attempt to confuse the defenders, Rubensdorffer decided to take on Kenley from the north, but found himself over the southern suburbs of London – Hitler had forbidden all attacks on the British capital – so the Me 110s turned south.

'Sooner than expected,' wrote Bekker, 'the airfield lay ahead and the Me 110s went down to attack. Suddenly Hurricanes appeared above but failed to get close because in a dive the heavy Messerschmitts were faster. Their bombs slammed into hangars, and at least forty training planes were destroyed. Others struck two camouflaged aircraft and aero-engine works. Still others severely damaged a factory producing aircraft radio sets. None of this, however, took place at Kenley, but at the London airfield of Croydon. Rubensdorffer had made a navigational error!'

Croydon airfield and the surrounding town were scenes of devastation: four British airmen and sixty-two civilians were killed. Another 185 were injured. It was the first time during the war that bombs had fallen on Greater London.

In the air, fortunes changed swiftly. As Rubensdorffer's men pulled away, they were confronted by two squadrons of Hurricanes and tried to form a defensive circle south of the town. As with so

60

many accounts of fast-moving aerial fighting at the time, there is some confusion over what happened next, but it appears as though Rubensdorffer's aircraft was attacked twice.

The first assault is likely to have involved Squadron Leader John Thompson of III Squadron, who recalled events in 1983 when he was interviewed by the aviation historian John Vasco, who wrote a history of Rubensdorffer's unit.

'We saw the bombers just after they had entered their dive east of the airfield. We turned in immediately to engage. I chose the leader and caught him climbing vertically after his attack. I remember seeing my bullets striking his fuselage and wings, but could not stay to see what happened as I was being approached by a 109.'

If it was Rubensdorffer's aircraft that Thompson damaged, the Swiss airman broke away and with four other aircraft from his flight headed for the Channel. But he was already in trouble. He told one of his Bf 109 pilots over the radio that his gunner, Senior Lance-Corporal Ludwig Kretzer, was dead and that he, Rubensdorffer, was wounded.

Flying south of Tunbridge Wells, Rubensdorffer came under fire again. Pilot Officer Ron Duckenfield, flying a Hurricane with 501 Squadron, recalled seeing an enemy aircraft in the area flying south in a long shallow dive towards the coast.

Nearly forty years later, Duckenfield wrote: 'I fired several bursts with no apparent effect – he was weaving pretty violently – but then, when we were both down to about 4,000ft, I managed to hit him with the last of my ammunition. One engine caught fire.' Duckenfield identified the enemy aircraft as a Dornier 2015, but in all likelihood it was Rubensdorffer's Jabo.

Another witness was George Tuke, a sixteen-year-old who had gone to the cinema in Tunbridge Wells with his parents and was on his way home by bus. 'At Trulls Hatch we were met by the raised hand of a police officer or a warden directing the bus into a layby under the trees,' he said. 'Everyone was ordered off the bus to take cover.'

The boy walked across the road to a ditch near a field gate and heard gunfire to the north. 'My attention was suddenly drawn to what can only be described as a ball of black smoke, flecked with puffs of red, coming at a very low height towards me. [It was] obviously an aircraft in dire trouble . . . in an instant, it dived into the ground, followed a few seconds later by a pent-up explosion and towering pall of smoke and flame.'

Tuke soon 'realised that the aircraft was an Me 110, which normally carried a crew of a pilot and gunner. Amidst all of this were their now crumpled bodies.'

Rubensdorffer had crashed on the site of a pig farm near Rotherfield. His aircraft was one of seven lost by his unit on 15 August, which the Luftwaffe called 'Black Thursday'. The British claimed that 182 German aircraft had been destroyed during the day. The real total was seventy-six, but this was bad enough. The RAF lost thirty-six.

When Rubensdorffer's body was removed, a telegram was found in his pocket. It was from Kesselring, the head of Air Fleet 2, congratulating him on the award of the Iron Cross, First Class for 'courageous leadership'. Four days later, he became the first pilot of a Messerschmitt 110 to be posthumously awarded the Knight's Cross of the Iron Cross, one of the highest honours in Nazi Germany.

Rubensdorffer's instruction that his ashes be scattered from an aeroplane was never realised. He was buried with his gunner in Tunbridge Wells. His body was later transferred to the German Military Cemetery at Cannock Chase in Staffordshire: block 9, row 4, grave 20.

Philip Hunter leading a flight of three Defiants, with their distinctive turrets.
The aircraft was used to great effect over Dunkirk, but had no forward-firing
guns and was vulnerable against German fighters

7

Squadron Leader Philip Hunter
Boulton Paul Defiant Turret Fighter

22 August 1940

His brilliant leadership as well as his example
and courage are of the highest standard.

A FTER ENJOYING CONSIDERABLE success in the air battles over
Dunkirk in late May and early June in 1940, Philip Hunter
and his 264 Squadron spent several weeks out of the front line,
flying their two-seater interceptors – Boulton Paul Defiants – from
airfields in Yorkshire and Scotland.

On 22 August, however, they were transferred to Hornchurch
in Essex, in the cauldron of the Battle of Britain, as part of a rota-
tion system in which the RAF tried to give its hard-pressed pilots
some respite from the appalling pressures of combat flying over
south-east England. A twenty-seven-year-old ace in the now
almost-forgotten Defiants, Squadron Leader Hunter thus became
one of Churchill's 'Few'.

In a speech to Parliament two days before Hunter's move to
Hornchurch, the redoubtable British prime minister repeated a
sentence that he had been heard to say to himself in a car taking
him from the headquarters of 11 Group at Uxbridge back to London:
'Never in the field of human conflict was so much owed by so
many to so few.'

Only part of that address, which dealt mainly with the war against
the Italians in Africa, referred to Fighter Command and its pilots
– but Churchill's words defined their place in history.

At fighter bases such as Hornchurch, the British leader's words
were turned into a joke about mess bills. Yet elsewhere many knew

that the fate of Western civilisation was being decided in the skies above Kent and Sussex and that the toll on pilots was severe.

At this stage in mid-August, the full weight of the German air force was being brought to bear on the structure of Britain's air defences: fighter stations, radar installations, aircraft factories, supply lines and RAF communications were all on the list of Luftwaffe targets.

Ranging over the length and breadth of the British Isles, the Luftwaffe bombed Scotland and the north-east of England from bases in Denmark and Norway. The Luftwaffe also targeted Portsmouth, Southampton, oil storage tanks close to Pembroke Docks in Wales, and aircraft works at Filton in Bristol and Norwich, Hull and Bradford.

The Germans bombed the capital on 22 August. At 3.30 a.m., Harrow and Wealdstone, which came within Civil Defence Area 5 – classified as London – came under attack. British civilians on the ground largely held their nerve in the face of the bombing, but the expectation of invasion was widespread, and it was at this moment that Fighter Command came closest to losing the Battle of Britain.

Both sides were suffering greatly. Casualty records for the RAF from 6 August to 2 September show losses of 444 aircraft, including 410 Spitfires and Hurricanes. German records detail the loss of 443 fighters between 8 August and 31 August, with total losses of about 900 front-line aircraft.

The figures underline that two types of aircraft suffered particularly badly. On the German side, the Junkers 87 Stuka, the most accurate weapon in the German armoury and the most effective against radar stations, was withdrawn from the battle on 18 August, because it was too slow and thus too easy a target for British fighters. The same fate later befell the Boulton Paul Defiant, but for different reasons.

Known to its pilots as the 'Daffy', the Defiant was a classic example of a war machine that was soon found to be inadequate to its task. In the late 1920s and early 1930s, the Air Ministry imagined that Britain might come under attack by the Germans in a future war. However, strategists believed that the attacks would be prosecuted by bombers unaccompanied by fighter escorts, which would not have the range to reach the British mainland from German airfields.

They had not foreseen that Hitler would quickly overrun France and be able to launch airborne assaults across the Channel from French airfields, so that bombers and fighters could fly together.

The Defiant was built by the Boulton Paul Aircraft company in Wolverhampton and designed by its chief engineer, John Dudley North, to a specification laid down by the Air Ministry for a turret-armed defensive fighter. It was conceived to destroy bombers and carried its only armament in a hydraulically powered revolving turret at the top of the fuselage. This was occupied by a gunner sitting just behind the pilot's cockpit.

The plane had no forward-facing armament – nothing in its wings – and the four Browning machine guns in the turret were intended for use on targets primarily behind or above it. They could not be used against an enemy fighter approaching head-on.

Over Dunkirk and in the early stages of the Battle of Britain, RAF pilots used Defiants to considerable effect against German bombers and some fighters. At that point in the war, Luftwaffe pilots often mistook the Defiants for Hurricanes, because the Defiant's fuselage was similar to the more famous fighter. As a result of that error, the German pilots would try to 'bounce' the Defiants from behind – as they would Spitfires and Hurricanes – only to expose themselves to withering fire from the turret gunner.

However, once Goering's airmen learnt to spot the turret, the Boulton Paul Defiant was doomed as a daylight-operating interceptor and it started to be shot down in large numbers. The losses mounted during the summer despite clever tactics by its squadrons: the planes flew in circular formations to stop German fighters picking individual planes off and Defiants were mixed in with Hurricanes and Spitfires to make them harder to spot.

The Defiants were not only poorly armed for daylight engagements; they were also slow in comparison with Spitfires and Hurricanes, and indeed Messerschmitt Bf 109s, because of the extra weight added by the turret. For the air gunners, the Defiant proved a particularly dangerous aircraft because, while the pilots were usually able to bail out after contact with the enemy, the gunners often became trapped in their turrets and were lost with the plane.

The gunners could not use normal parachute packs, but had to wear a 'rhino suit' due to the lack of space in the turret. This was like a huge overcoat containing the parachute and a dinghy and oars, but it made escaping – through the opened shell of the canopy over the turret or through a hole in the floor – very difficult in a plane that was possibly on fire and spinning out of control.

Philip Hunter was not merely an exceptionally gifted British pilot, he was a leader of men in battle, who believed in setting an example to his pilots and carrying out his own orders, no matter how daunting they were. A day after the move to Hornchurch, a newly qualified pilot who had recently joined 264 Squadron approached Hunter after dinner in the mess. There followed an exchange that hints at the underlying fear some Defiant pilots must have felt, knowing that they were going into battle in machinery that was likely to be outclassed by enemy fighters.

Pilot Officer James Bailey told his commanding officer over coffee that, in his view, it was quite wrong that Defiants should be selected for first patrols the following morning, given the shortcomings of the aircraft. The Daffy was, he explained to Hunter, a magnificent destroyer of bombers, but was 'a little helpless' against German fighters. 'We should be the last not the first, I argued,' recalled Bailey.

Hunter did not disagree on the performance of the Defiants, but he told Bailey that the squadron was 'in the place of honour' and must accept it.

There is some uncertainty as to the timing of operations the next day, but it is thought that on 24 August the squadron moved a few miles east to RAF Rochford, now the site of Southend airport.

That morning, the city of Portsmouth sustained the heaviest casualties yet inflicted in a single bombing raid; more than 100 people were killed and 300 injured. In Essex, Hunter's squadron was scrambled when the airfield at Manston in Kent, just across the Thames estuary from Rochford, was attacked by a force of Junkers 88s and Bf 109s.

Together with his air gunner, Pilot Officer Frederick H. King – although some reports suggest it was Pilot Officer Frederick Hill – Hunter took off in his Defiant and climbed to take on the German invaders. They were last seen at 12.40 p.m. pursuing a Junkers 88 at full throttle over the Channel. Neither man was heard of again. They were listed as missing in action and there is no record of what happened to them.

*Hunter with his son, Nigel; and,
nearest the fuselage, with his crews*

A gunner wearing a 'rhino suit'

Bailey's own recollection of that day – he did not fly because he was considered too inexperienced – was that the Defiants, including that of Hunter and King, had become 'trapped', as he put it, 'against the sea' by German fighters as they took off. This suggests that Hunter's Defiant had indeed been picked off by a Messerschmitt.

Hunter's widow, Eleanor, received a three-page handwritten letter of sympathy from Air Chief Marshal Trafford Leigh-Mallory, the Commanding Officer of 12 Group Fighter Command. He told her that her husband had been an outstanding RAF officer. 'I cannot tell you quite how much I admired Philip Hunter's efficiency and gallantry as a squadron commander,' he wrote. 'I regarded him as exceptional in every way and consider he is a very great loss to the service.'

Philip Algernon Hunter was the son of Captain Albert Hunter and his wife, Clara. He was born in April 1913 in Frimley, Surrey. He began his education at Junior King's School Canterbury, before moving to Rosslyn House School at Felixstowe and finally Bishop's Stortford School. Hunter was commissioned as an RAF probationary pilot officer in 1931, becoming a flying officer in 1933. He was posted to Egypt, where he flew the Fairey Gordon light bomber, a two-seater biplane.

When he returned to England in 1936, Hunter was granted a permanent commission as a flight lieutenant and joined the staff of the RAF College at Cranwell. He then moved to the Central Flying School at Upavon as a senior instructor and was promoted to squadron leader in December 1938. Hunter had a certain style about him and loved to drive his sports car, into which he would squeeze not only his future wife, but his two Great Danes as well.

A month after the Second World War began, in October 1939, Hunter was posted to command 254 Squadron, flying Bristol Blenheim twin-engine fighters from RAF Stradishall in Suffolk. But by March 1940 he had moved to take charge of 264 Squadron flying Defiants from RAF Martlesham Heath in Suffolk. At this stage the role of the Defiant was already uncertain and, while the crews got to grips with their new planes, there were extensive tests and tactical trials as the RAF worked out whether the two-seater could be used during the day and at night.

It was during this period that Hunter demonstrated his prowess as a pilot when, not long after taking command of 264 Squadron, he took part in a mock dogfight between a Defiant and a Spitfire at the Air Fighting Development Unit at RAF Northolt. The Spitfire put up against Hunter that day was flown by Flying Officer Robert Stanford Tuck of 65 Squadron, who would become one of the most celebrated British fighter pilots of the Second World War.

The report of the dogfight was compiled by a Wing Commander Hasse, who refers to a 'cine-gun' that, instead of firing bullets, filmed episodes when a plane opened fire:

> After some preliminary practice engagements, the Defiant was placed on a patrol line, and a Spitfire was instructed to attack when desired. The full initiative in the attack was therefore given to the Spitfire.
>
> As the Spitfire approached, the air gunner of the Defiant was able to open fire. The Defiant went into a steep turn and was followed by the Spitfire. The engagement lasted about ten minutes, and the air gunner after the first five minutes had used up all his film. During the whole engagement, the Spitfire was unable to bring his guns to bear and finally landed having failed to use his cine gun.

Hunter and his gunner had shown that they could outmanoeuvre a Spitfire and the Defiant pilot provided detailed notes on how his plane should be handled in close combat with a fighter. In the hands of less able pilots, however, the outcome would not be so positive.

In the build-up to, and during the evacuation from, Dunkirk, Hunter and King enjoyed a run of success. On 12 May they destroyed a Junkers 88 near the Hague, which crashed into a field of cows in the Netherlands, as described by Hunter in his typically brisk combat report:

> Took off from Horsham 13.10. Arrived at the Hague and commenced patrol at 13.55 hours. Saw an aircraft approach and drop one bomb on three destroyers at 14.10. Immediately after bombing, [it] turned [towards] the land at 5,000ft. I cut him off

with Red Section and gave the order No 1 attack GO. As he turned, he dived down to the ground forcing me to change over with No 3 to the starboard side. I could see my AG's [air gunner's] bullets hitting the aircraft, which finally crashed in a field with dykes around it and hundreds of cows at 14.15.

Once the evacuation of Dunkirk began on 26 May, Hunter and his squadron flew daily sorties over the beaches of northern France. On 27 May, Hunter and King shot down a Bf 109 and shared in the downing of a Heinkel 111. The next day they took down two Bf 109s.

Then came the extraordinary events of 29 May, when Hunter destroyed one Bf 109, one Me 110 and a Stuka in combat over Dunkirk and the Channel. That day his squadron shot down thirty-eight enemy aircraft during two action-packed patrols; the Defiants destroyed eighteen Stukas alone. Hunter and King had further successes on 31 May, when they shot down two planes and damaged a third.

For these actions Hunter was awarded the Distinguished Service Order, and King the Distinguished Flying Medal. Hunter's citation appeared in the *London Gazette* on 14 June: 'In May 1940, under the leadership of Squadron Leader Hunter, this squadron shot down thirty-eight enemy aircraft during the course of two patrols. He personally destroyed three of that number. His brilliant leadership as well as his example and courage are of the highest standard.'

After his death, Hunter was mentioned in dispatches in the *London Gazette* of 1 January 1941. Hunter's logbook and medals can be found at the Kent Battle of Britain Museum at Hawkinge, a former wartime aerodrome. He is commemorated at the Air Forces Memorial at Runnymede at Englefield Green in Surrey, which is reserved for those who were lost in the Second World War in air or other operations and who have no known grave.

Hunter's name can be seen on Panel 4, underneath that of Squadron Leader H.R.L. 'Robin' Hood, who went missing on 5 September 1940 while leading twelve Spitfires that had scrambled to intercept a large Luftwaffe formation flying up the Thames estuary.

Although the Defiants were largely withdrawn from daylight

operations in the autumn of 1940, they became effective night fighters and were used with considerable success in that role against German bombers after the Battle of Britain. They were also used for target towing, as high-speed gunnery training planes, in air-sea rescue and in the operation of electronic countermeasures. The Defiant was withdrawn from service in 1942, by which time 1,064 had been built.

Hunter left not only his young wife, who remarried, but also their newborn son. After being educated at Sherborne School, Nigel Hunter went on to become a distinguished consultant paediatrician at the Gloucestershire Royal Hospital.

His daughter, Sarah Nicholls, remembered that Nigel learnt to fly, inspired by the example of his father, but never had any intention of joining the RAF himself. In an intriguing clue as to the character and qualities of her grandfather, Sarah also remembered her parents receiving a letter from Derek Smythe, a former friend of Hunter's. He told the story of Pilot Officer S.R. Thomas, who was so impressed with Hunter that he named his son after him in 1940.

The crew of a Heinkel III running to their aircraft at a base in northern France in 1940. The bulbous-nosed bomber became a symbol of aerial aggression during the first years of the Second World War

8

Sergeant Ernst Wedding
Heinkel 111 Medium Bomber

24 August 1940

I was a boy, but you grow up very quickly,
especially when someone is after your skin.

MANY YEARS AFTER the Battle of Britain, Ernst Wedding, a sharp eighty-two-year-old veteran who had been a Luftwaffe bomber pilot, vividly recalled his first low-level mission against an RAF aerodrome. It was like 'watching a B movie', he said.

According to Wedding, the target was North Weald in Essex, one of the main air bases on which the defence of London depended, but this might not be correct. He recalled the raid being in September, but the date appears likely to have been Saturday, 24 August, although this is not certain. If it was that day, most of the cloud had cleared by dawn; conditions were favourable for bombing.

Based at an airfield at Chartres, the great cathedral city southwest of Paris, Wedding flew a Heinkel 111, a distinctive twin-engine German bomber with a bulbous glazed nose, and the bright red propeller cones of the Luftwaffe 'battle-wing' KG55. He was briefed about the target on the morning of the raid. Every squadron in KG55 – there were twelve, each with nine aircraft – was given a specific airfield to attack. For Wedding's squadron, it was apparently North Weald, thirty miles north-east of London.

Waves of bombers were detected heading towards London after 3 p.m., according to the Battle of Britain Historical Society, but then they changed course, which took them in a straight line for North Weald and another of the RAF's key airfields, Hornchurch. Both aerodromes 'suffered considerable damage'. Living quarters, stores and messes were destroyed, as well as several aircraft on the ground, but the airfields remained operational.

'It was the first time that I did a low-level attack on an airfield,' Wedding said. 'The heaviest bomb we were carrying would be 50kg – hundred pounders – and we had a lot of machine gun ammunition, more than usual. Normally on a Heinkel 111 you had 750 rounds per gun, but on that day we had 1,500 rounds per gun, so we could do damage with the machine guns. As we got to North Weald, we turned the runway over.'

Asked sixty-four years later what images of the battle remained with him, the German pilot said: 'When you dropped your bombs you saw the smoke coming up, people running around, vehicles turning over, setting on fire. It was just, how shall I say, like a B movie. It seemed to be unreal, [but] it was real all right.'

Long before his twentieth birthday, Wedding was already an experienced pilot. His unit took part in the Luftwaffe's campaigns in Poland and France, and flew throughout the Battle of Britain, from the first actions over the Channel against British convoys to the night-time bombing of cities in the Blitz.

Looking back, Wedding recalled: 'I was a boy . . . but you grow up very quickly, especially when someone is after your skin.'

His unit played a prominent role in the German attempt to destroy the RAF in the summer of 1940. In directives issued by the Luftwaffe, Goering made it clear that the air force's task was to break Fighter Command. 'The enemy is to be forced to use his fighters by means of ceaseless attacks,' Goering ordered. 'These fighters must be destroyed if we are to succeed.'

He also emphasised the need to destroy the RAF's infrastructure and airfields and the British aircraft industry. All were to be attacked night and day, by individual aircraft if weather conditions hampered big formations.

Much depended on the Heinkel 111 – and young men such as Wedding. The aircraft was designed in the mid-1930s by Siegfried and Walter Gunter, who were working for Ernst Heinkel, an aviation pioneer – and Nazi party member – at his factory at Warnemunde on the Baltic. From the outset, the plane was described as *ein wolf im schafspelz* (a wolf in sheep's clothing); it was 'disguised' as an airliner to overcome restrictions imposed on German armaments by the victors of the First World War under the Treaty of Versailles.

While the Heinkel III first flew in 1935 and several were soon in service with the national airline, Deutsche Lufthansa, the aircraft had been built with military roles in mind and it would prove to be a remarkably versatile machine.

The many variants were denoted by different letters of the alphabet and went on to be used as bombers, pathfinders, reconnaissance planes, for transport and resupply, and as a torpedo anti-shipping aircraft. The Heinkel was also used as a paratroop carrier, balloon cutter, glider tug – and in 1944 as an aerial platform for the launch of VI flying bombs.

The first military version of the He III had a machine gun in the nose, and rear-firing guns in pods on the upper fuselage and underside. The aircraft was quickly upgraded, however, and the Heinkel IIIB, with more powerful engines, was ready to fly with the German Condor Legion in support of Franco's nationalist forces during the Spanish Civil War.

Two of the aircraft were involved in the bombing of the Basque market town of Guernica on 26 April 1937, where hundreds of civilians are believed to have died, and which was later portrayed in Picasso's famous painting.

Indeed, the Heinkel III would become a symbol of aerial aggression during the first year of the Second World War. It was used in the bombing of Warsaw in September 1939 and a force of a hundred took part in the attack on Rotterdam in May 1940, which at the time was the most destructive raid in history.

By the start of the Battle of Britain, the Luftwaffe was using a new variant: the long-range Heinkel IIIH, which had a top speed of 270 mph, and could carry a bombload of up to 4,400lb to targets 720 miles away. The aircraft was also equipped with the latest electronic navigation and target-finding aids. Developed by the German firm Telefunken in the 1930s, these devices used radio beams to direct the bombers to their targets and, in the right conditions, could achieve great accuracy. The RAF had nothing similar until late 1941, although their scientists eventually succeeded in blocking the German beams.

In some aircraft, the crew was increased from four to five because of extra armaments, with one cannon in the nose and seven machine guns. In addition, the Heinkel could withstand considerable punishment.

For his part, Wedding had always been passionate about becoming a pilot. 'The appeal of flying is that you are free from the Earth,' he said, 'your horizon is unlimited. On a clear day you can see 90, 100, 110 miles. Today you are tied by radar. Well, we weren't. Once the wireless operator had signed off from the airfield, you were on your own. It was a terrific feeling to be free of everything.'

In an interview recorded for the Imperial War Museum (IWM) in 2004, Wedding told his story in fluent, precise English. 'It all started when I was eighteen years old,' he said. 'When the war finished, I was twenty-three. An old man!'

Asked what it was like to fly a bomber in 1940, he compared it to 'driving a bus'. The most important task for a pilot was to keep his place in the formation, whether it was big or small. Such discipline was tedious, he said, but essential to survival.

When the fighters attacked, the bombers needed to be close together so they could concentrate their fire power. 'You can't do any mad manoeuvres within the formation, because if you did you would crash into your own aircraft . . . you are watching the aircraft in front of you and the aircraft on your left and on your right and you're hoping the chap besides you does the same.

'A bomber pilot had to be very steady. He couldn't afford to get nervous and twitchy. A fighter pilot could get rid of his anxieties by doing intricate manoeuvres, which you couldn't do with a bomber. For instance,' said Wedding, 'I couldn't fly a loop with a bomber. No, impossible. So I just had to sit there and take what was coming and hope that my gunners and the gunners from other bombers would keep us safe.'

He added: 'You saw aircraft going nose down, trailing smoke. You see parachutes opening, crew bailing out. Then you see the aircraft crashing in a great plume of fire and smoke. Some aircraft trail smoke, but still manage to get home; one engine shot out or even half the tail shot away, but still made it home . . . then it was a question of who was wounded from the crews? Or who got killed? . . . After a while some of the old faces disappeared and new faces came and then the new faces disappeared. It was a constant fluctuation of the crews.'

Wedding survived, however. He admitted that there were times when he was afraid, though they all had fears, he said.

'But through training we mastered the fear. If fear takes over, you're lost. You are no good to anybody, even to yourself. So if you can surprise the fear and control it, then you will be all right. And by other crew members backing you up, then your fear disappears. Yes, you will be anxious. If you weren't, you wouldn't be any good, because that keeps you alert and that keeps you alive.'

The North Weald attack was Wedding's only combat mission that day and he returned safely with his crew to Chartres, which was farther from the target than many of the other German airfields in Nazi-occupied Western Europe.

On that day the Luftwaffe had mounted six significant raids. Manston aerodrome on the Kent coast was abandoned by the RAF as a forward base after repeated attacks and was thereafter used only for emergency landings. Large formations were seen over Ramsgate, where 1,200 houses were destroyed, then Dover and along the Thames estuary. Casualties and fatalities in Portsmouth were high after another prolonged attack.

As day turned to night, a hundred German bombers took off with the apparent aim of attacking the Short aircraft factory at Rochester, the oil storage facility at Thameshaven and other targets across London: Croydon, Banstead, Lewisham, Uxbridge, Stepney, Harrow and Hayes all suffered damage. Two aircraft, both He 111s, dropped their loads on Oxford Street, which was the first time that bombs had fallen on central London since 1918.

While neither Hitler nor Goering ordered this attack on the city centre, which has been widely blamed on a navigational error, the Luftwaffe had been encroaching on London for some time. The date usually given for the start of the bombing campaign against the British capital is 7 September; the reality is that by then areas of the city had been under attack for at least three weeks.

During the course of the war, Wedding claimed to have seen both Nazi leaders, Hitler and Goering, while he was serving on the Eastern Front, where he is believed to have flown as a courier pilot. Hitler visited units of KG55, which was based at one point close to the Fuhrer's headquarters at Vinnytsia in the Ukraine.

According to Wedding: 'The man had something; I can't explain what it was, but he had some magnetism which drew attention to him straight away . . . he had a certain penetrating look . . . it didn't send a shiver to you, but it certainly made you alert.' He also saw Goering, but was critical of him. 'He played too much politics rather than looking after the air force.'

In an opinion voiced by other German airmen after the war, Wedding was adamant that the crews were not fighting for Hitler or Goering. 'We were flying for Germany and the air force,' he said.

He remained proud of his comrades, particularly his own crews, and the sense of brotherly discipline in their bomber. 'You take care of them and they take care of you. The crew of any aircraft is tighter-knit than the family, because each depends on the next one about his life.'

He defended the German fighter pilots. 'They were just as good as the British pilots . . . and they had the same attitude, to knock the enemy out of the sky and to protect their own formations.'

He liked the meritocratic nature of the Luftwaffe, too. 'Once you were on the airfield there were no ranks. You didn't salute any more, you didn't call anyone "sir". Ranks completely disappeared. It was Tom, Dick and Harry; in our case Hans, Fritz and Oscar.' And Wedding admired their team spirit. 'The morale never suffered, the morale was still there even in the dark days of 1944 and 1945,' he said.

So what went wrong for the Luftwaffe in the summer of 1940?

Wedding admired Air Chief Marshal Sir Hugh Dowding, the head of Fighter Command. 'I only knew he was commander in chief of the RAF and that was it. Otherwise he wasn't discussed, because we had enough of our own blokes to discuss,' Wedding said, chuckling. Later on, though, he came to the conclusion that Dowding was 'a very cool, calculated leader of the RAF'. Dowding was right, Wedding believed, to withhold men and machines from the Battle of France and nurture them for the defence of Britain.

The former bomber pilot also raised the issue of radar, which he believed played a key role in the outcome of the battle. The RAF 'didn't need to fly standard patrols. They could conserve fuel . . . and flying time. Because at any given time they knew exactly where the attacking forces were, which strength, which direction

*A formation of He 111s;
Ernst Wedding on British
television in later life; and
a bomber over London*

they were flying, so at the last moment they could send up aircraft to intercept us, and they had the shortest approach time necessary to get into a fighting position, that was half the battle . . . radar did it for the RAF.'

In Wedding's view, the Nazi leadership also played a significant role in the outcome. 'The original plan was to knock out the RAF, which we could have done if Hitler had not changed his mind halfway through the Battle of Britain,' Wedding said. 'Because of the losses sustained [by] the RAF and its pilots, they couldn't have enough pilots . . . if he [Hitler] hadn't changed tactics [and started attacking London and the cities], I think by the end of October 1940 the RAF would have been completely grounded. If we had kept on, as we started, the RAF would have been beaten.'

By the early summer of 1941, KG55 had been transferred from its bases in France to eastern Europe in support of Operation Barbarossa, the German invasion of the Soviet Union. Wedding seems to have spent much of the rest of the war in Ukraine and Russia, where the unit's missions included attempts to resupply Von Paulus's sixth army at Stalingrad.

By the last year of the war, Wedding was apparently flying in defence of the homeland against the vast numbers of Allied bombers attacking Germany; the Americans in daylight and the British at night. In early 1945, he was shot down over Germany by an American P38 twin-engine fighter known as the 'Lightning'. It is not known what aircraft he was flying. Wedding's wireless operator was seriously wounded. 'I got away without a scratch,' he said. 'I was lucky.'

After the German surrender, Wedding was sent to a 'quarantine camp' in Nebraska in the United States. 'The only sounds we could hear were from the railway engine or the prairie dogs nattering at night,' he said.

In 2000, Wedding gave an interview to the historian John Hughes-Wilson as part of a BBC1 programme called *What If: The Battle of Britain*, which looked at Hitler's plans for the invasion of Britain and how Operation Sealion would have progressed had Fighter Command been defeated by the Luftwaffe. He also appeared in the BBC programme *War Walks*, series two, episode six, and the Channel 4 documentary *Spitfire Ace*.

He later gave his interview to the IWM, which was recorded by the Bristol-based production company RDF Media. The interview is compelling – vivid at times, with astute observations, touches of humour, and no hint of bombast.

Yet there are inconsistencies with what is known about the battle, which is not unusual in the recollections of veterans in old age, but these should be noted. Wedding says the attack on North Weald was on 15 September, but there were no attacks on RAF airfields that day. North Weald was heavily attacked in a raid similar to the one described by Wedding on 24 August. But there is also no record of KG55 operating against North Weald, which would have been an unlikely target for a unit flying out of Chartres.

More than ten years after including Wedding in its archive of oral histories, the IWM appears to have no record of the man. Only his recorded voice, it seems, is left to tell his story of the Battle of Britain – and the accuracy of his narrative cannot be confirmed.

Wedding is not mentioned in any books about KG55 and there has been no response to inquiries on German military websites. He does not appear to have been decorated by the Nazi state, in spite of flying almost continuously from the first day of the war until the last.

He has, however, been quoted by authors and historians in many British books, including *Spitfire to Reaper: The Changing Face of Aerial Warfare* and books on the Battle of Britain by Patrick Bishop and Kate Moore. He is also quoted widely in Joshua Levine's *Forgotten Voices of the Blitz and the Battle of Britain*.

Further inquiries through RDF Media, however, eventually established a few more personal details. He was born Ernst August Gustav Wedding in 1920. After a period as a prisoner of war, he married an English woman, Barbara Beacon, and appears to have changed his first name to Ernest. The couple had a son.

The story does not end there, though; a few years before that, the aviation historian Chris Goss, who specialises in the Luftwaffe, believes he came across Ernest Wedding after giving a speech to a branch of the RAF Association in west London. Wedding was in the audience. It seems that he gave regular talks and was living in Uxbridge – which was one of the areas of London bombed by the Luftwaffe on 24 August 1940. He died in 2007.

The New Zealander Neil Svendsen at the controls of a single-engine Fairey Battle. As the pilot of a twin-engine Hampden, he flew on Bomber Command's first raid against the German capital, Berlin

9

Flying Officer Neil H. Svendsen
Handley Page Hampden Medium Bomber

25 August 1940

God willing, I should come through this scrap OK
and I hope without a broken body.

WHEN FLYING OFFICER Neil Svendsen ran out of fuel and crash-landed his Handley Page Hampden bomber in the Wash, off the coast of Lincolnshire, in the early hours of 26 August 1940, it marked the end of an extraordinary feat of aviation. His mission with 83 Squadron on that day also marked the beginning of an Allied military strategy that would culminate in the destruction of Dresden and many other German cities over the next five years.

The RAF was embarking on the strategic bombing of Germany – and Svendsen's aircraft was one of about seventy to eighty twin-engine bombers ordered to retaliate after the Luftwaffe had 'accidentally' attacked central London on the night of 24 August. Whether the German raid on the British capital was deliberate or not, Churchill put into action a plan he had been working on with his military chiefs for some weeks – the bombing of Berlin.

The raid was of far greater range than the many missions flown by Svendsen, a quiet New Zealander of Danish descent. He was 5ft 7in tall with dark brown hair, and was described as a good listener. He had also already won the Distinguished Flying Cross. In a letter to his mother, Ada, posted earlier that summer, Svendsen gave a vivid description of life with Bomber Command – and the fears of those on the ground in Britain.

'Everybody is expecting England to be invaded at any time,' he wrote on 16 June, 'and it is almost impossible to get anywhere without having to show an identity card or something. The war in France seems to be going pretty badly for us due to the inability of the Allied troops to deal with the German tanks, which just go where they please . . .'

He continued: 'No doubt you have been wondering what I have been doing in this war. Well, I must say I have, with the rest of the squadron, been pretty busy.'

By this stage Svendsen had flown fourteen night-time missions over enemy territory, all taking between five and seven hours. On the first nine trips he had flown as second pilot, but on the last five he had been the pilot, or as he proudly told his mother, 'captain of the machine'.

He also informed her of the RAF's first big raid on Hamburg:

Nearly seventy machines from different stations went over that night, each carrying a ton of bombs so you can guess at the damage done. I was in one of the machines as second pilot navigator and bomb aimer.

It was a lovely night and when we got to the German coast, we could see the oil tanks burning ninety miles away. We were the last to attack the target and all the way there from the German coast we were under quite heavy AA [anti-aircraft] fire. However, when we got to the target the shells just seem[ed] to come at us from all directions and it is still a miracle to me how we weren't hit . . .

We did one run on the target which we could see quite well and dropped our bombs (four of them). The bombs all fell in the centre of the area and one hit a big storage tank, which went up with a terrific burst of flame and started a third big fire in the area.

Svendsen told his mother of several other 'trips' that took them close to the large industrial areas of the Ruhr valley where 'our job was to bomb trains especially, or troops moving on roads'. He said that they had hit two stationary goods trains in a cutting, but admitted that his first missions in charge of the aircraft were not so successful. His new navigator, he said, was 'not so hot'.

He also voiced concern for his parents. 'I don't want you to get the "wind up" after reading this, which is all quite true incidentally and not exaggerated at all,' but then he added: 'I think, God willing, I should come through this scrap OK and I hope without a broken body.'

On October 23, two nights before the attack on Berlin, Svendsen had flown his Hampden against German 'invasion' forces. A report in the National Archive, based on Svendsen's debriefing with intelligence officers at his base at Scampton in Lincolnshire, states: 'Successful. Attacked and hit barges at Brest seaplane base, with bombs.'

News of the planned attack on Berlin was greeted enthusiastically at RAF bomber bases, particularly among the crews of 83 Squadron at Scampton. Svendsen's fellow pilots included Guy Gibson, who would win the Victoria Cross leading the 'Dambusters' raid three years later.

In his autobiography, *Enemy Coast Ahead*, Gibson wrote: 'We had been waiting for this for a long time. Now we were going to get our chance. Many pilots who had been given an off-night immediately began to plead to have themselves put down on the list of the first crews to bomb the German capital.'

While the Luftwaffe had already attacked many cities across Europe, the Nazi leadership had claimed that Berlin was invulnerable. Indeed, Goering had told an audience the previous September: 'If one enemy bomb falls on Berlin, you can call me Meyer [one of the most common names in Germany]!'

Not for the first time, the flamboyant leader of the Luftwaffe was guilty of hubris. After the RAF had proved him wrong, many Germans took to referring to air-raid alarms as 'Meyer's trumpets'.

For Svendsen, then aged twenty-five, the mission began shortly after sunset. Settled into his cramped cockpit, he increased the flow of fuel to the Hampden's Bristol Pegasus engines and rolled down the expansive grass runway at Scampton. With a full load of bombs and fuel, the aeroplane felt heavy on take-off and picked up speed only after some time in the air. After a few minutes, Svendsen's navigator set a course over Lincoln Cathedral a few miles away, taking the aircraft eastwards over the North Sea.

Named after Sir John Hampden, a seventeenth-century politician renowned for his defence of civil liberties, Svendsen's aircraft was more commonly known as the 'flying suitcase' by its four-man crews, because of the cramped conditions on board. Indeed, by 1940, the much-derided Handley Page Hampden was already virtually obsolete.

The aircraft was one of three long-range bombers in service with Bomber Command in September 1939; the other two were the Armstrong Whitworth Whitley and the Vickers Wellington. The Hampden originated from a 1932 Air Ministry specification that sought a bomber with a higher performance than any previously built for the RAF.

Designed at the Handley Page company in Hertfordshire by a team under G.R. Vokert, the Hampden was a modern all-metal aircraft, with a big, semicircular clear nose, a 53ft fuselage that was just 3ft wide, and a wingspan of 69ft. It had a cruising speed of 155 mph and a relatively fast top speed for the day of about 240 mph.

The aircraft could carry a bomb load of 4,000lb, and had a maximum range of 1,200 miles. The distance between Scampton and the German capital is almost exactly 600 miles.

The four-man crew was made up of a pilot, a second pilot who was also the navigator and bomb aimer, a specialist air gunner, and a radio operator who doubled up as a gunner. To defend themselves, they had a single Browning machine gun in the nose, and machine guns in a mid-upper position and in the belly of the aircraft.

First flown on 24 June 1938, the prototype Hampden took off from Radlett aerodrome in Hertfordshire in the presence of Lady Katharine Mary Montagu Douglas Scott, otherwise known as Viscountess Hampden. The man at the controls that day was Handley Page's chief test pilot, J.L.H.B. Cordes.

Three months later, 49 Squadron received the first operational Hampdens. More than 200 were in service with ten squadrons by the outbreak of war.

Although the Air Ministry had been looking for a radical new design, the specification was older than its German counterparts; it lacked modern navigation aids and other equipment and was easy prey for contemporary German fighters in daylight.

According to one former pilot, Wilfred Lewis, who flew his first

*Svendsen leaving Buckingham
Palace after receiving his DFC*

*Hampdens before
and after raids*

tour of operations on Hampdens, it was 'a beautiful aeroplane to fly, terrible to fly in! Cramped, no heat, no facilities where you could relieve yourself [although 'pee tubes' were used by some airmen]. You got in there and you were stuck there,' he said.

Svendsen does not appear to have recorded his opinions of the aircraft, but he succeeded in reaching Berlin, or at least somewhere in the region of the German capital. It was a remarkable piece of flying by the New Zealander, whose journey that night was the longest in terms of operational endurance recorded by a Hampden: ten hours and forty minutes. But the mission did not go exactly to plan.

In an interview given after the war, Svendsen recalled the events of 25 August 1940. 'We reached the target area OK,' he said, 'but as the cloud cover was 10/10 we had little chance of identifying it, so we set [off] for home intending to bomb the Luftwaffe air base on Texel [off the Dutch coast].'

After nine and a half hours' flying, Svendsen reached the coast, but could not find Texel. 'From a wireless bearing we obtained from Scampton, our home base, we found we were many miles north, off track, as the wind had swung 180 degrees since we left Berlin . . . I knew we would be lucky to get home on the petrol we had and, sure enough, the motors started spluttering soon after we left the coast. I told the crew to prepare for a landing on the sea, but we managed to extend our glide for quite a way as Sergeant Barber, my wireless operator, kept signalling base that we were going down.'

After ten hours and forty minutes in the air, with the aircraft at 1,000ft, he saw two ships close together and decided to try to land near them. One of the ships then opened fire, but missed.

According to Svendsen: 'We hit the water, tail first, at about 60 mph and as the aircraft fell into the sea the two engines were wrenched off. There was quite a swell running, but we shipped only a little water, and had time to lift the dinghy out of the fuse-lage and throw it into the water, where it inflated. Then four of us stepped into it without even getting wet!'

The crew had landed close to a boat laying navigation buoys, and they were picked up by the naval escort that had fired at their aircraft. After a 'boozy night' at Harwich Naval Station, they returned to Scampton, where the officer commanding 5 Group, Arthur

Harris, later known as 'Bomber' Harris and head of Bomber Command, was waiting to question Svendsen.

'Did I think Berlin was too distant a target for Hampdens, he wanted to know,' recalled Svendsen. '"No, sir," I said, "not as long as the wind doesn't change while we're in the air." He seemed satisfied with that and sent us off on a week's leave.'

The incident also earned Svendsen and his crew the distinction of becoming members of the Goldfish Club, which is open only to those who have crash-landed an aircraft on water.

The results of that first raid on the German capital were not exactly impressive. Although Bomber Command's records are not clear on the precise number of aircraft sent to various targets that night, *The Bomber Command War Diaries*, by Martin Middlebrook and Clive Everitt, records that 103 planes took part in operations, about half of which were Hampdens and Wellingtons.

'Berlin was found to be covered by thick cloud, which prevented accurate bombing, and a strong headwind was encountered on the return flight. The Hampdens were at the limit of their fuel capacity in such conditions and three of them were lost and three more ditched in the sea on their return flight,' reported Middlebrook and Everitt.

'The only bombs falling within the city limits of Berlin destroyed a wooden summer house in a garden in the suburb of Rosenthal and two people were slightly injured. The Berlin records show that many bombs were dropped in the country areas south of the city and that some of these fell into large farms – *Stadtguter* – owned by the city of Berlin. A joke went round, "Now they are trying to starve us out!"'

The impact on Hitler and the Nazi leadership, however, was profound. It enraged the Fuhrer, who decided to retaliate. Two weeks later, on 7 September, the Germans abandoned their attacks on the RAF airfields and infrastructure, and started the relentless bombing of London and other British cities.

As the historian A.J.P. Taylor wrote in his book *The Second World War*: 'It also began, though no one appreciated this, the indiscriminate bombing of cities that was to continue throughout the war.'

Neil Hyland Svendsen had been born on the other side of the world, in Grey Street, Pukekohe, fifty miles south of Auckland, on

27 January 1915. He was the son of Herbert Neil Svendsen, whose family had emigrated from Denmark in the 1870s, and his wife, Ada Jane. He had three brothers and three sisters: Gordon, Fred and Les; and Elma, Olive and Merle.

He grew up in the small town, which was renowned for its market gardening and a racecourse, and was educated at Pukekohe primary school. On his way there, he would help to deliver milk from the family's dairy farm, using a horse and cart and ladling it out for his neighbours from churns.

Joining the scouts at the age of twelve, Svendsen became a King's Scout, achieving the highest award in the troop. On leaving Pukekohe technical high school in 1931, he worked on the family farm, signed up for the Volunteer Territorials, a kind of citizen's army, and started thinking about joining the RAF.

He enlisted in his home town in 1937, just as the Nazis were mounting a robust challenge to the new order that had been imposed on Europe by the Treaty of Versailles in 1919. The business of rearming had started in earnest, and German forces were already testing out their new weaponry in the Spanish Civil War.

Arriving in England at Southampton later that year, Svendsen trained as a pilot at the elementary flying school at Ansty in Warwickshire from September to November 1937, and was then accepted by the RAF as an acting pilot officer. 'Everything is going very well with me here,' he wrote in a letter home, 'and I am enjoying life immensely.' He continued his training at Tern Hill in Shropshire until June 1938, shortly before the Munich crisis.

When Britain declared war against Germany in September 1939, Svendsen was serving with 185 Squadron, which was part of Bomber Command, and equipped with Hampdens, Herefords and Ansons. He was transferred to 83 Squadron at Scampton in October 1939 and took part in raids on targets in France and Germany, as well as mine-laying, which was euphemistically referred to by the RAF as 'gardening'.

He was awarded the DFC in June 1940 after a mine-laying sortie in German waters. A flak ship pumped a shell into the nose of his Hampden, which blinded his navigator, who had doubled as his bomb aimer. Svendsen dropped the mine on his own and flew the aircraft home. He later told his mother:

I am ever so pleased you and Dad are getting so much publicity over my new 'gong'. I was very pleased when I got it, because I knew it would indicate to you that I hadn't been wasting my time over here. The knowledge that I am bringing honour to your name means infinitely more to me than just personal pride and if ever a son should strive to be worthy of his parents, I should strive to be worthy of you and Dad.

After the raid on Berlin, Svendsen recovered from his brush with the cold waters of the North Sea, and continued flying operations over Nazi-occupied Europe. On 6 September, he bombed an aerodrome in the Netherlands; he attacked unidentified targets on 9 September – 'No results observed owing to intense searchlight and anti-aircraft activity' – and laid mines on 11 September. 'Veg planted successfully. Bombs dropped on flak battery at Neowork.'

His name stands out – as does that of Gibson – in the squadron record book because of the initials DFC that follow them. On 18 September, they are listed, one after the other, after another attack on the invasion barges. Svendsen reports: 'Target identified and attacked.' Flying Officer Gibson states: 'On first attack, a heavy shell passed through cockpit by rudder bar, and rendered intercom U/S. Bombs dropped by Pilot.'

Svendsen flew throughout the Battle of Britain, then spent several months as an instructor. He started his second tour of operations in 1941. On the night of 30 June, his Hampden was hit by flak while on a raid over the Ruhr. The starboard engine was damaged and the aircraft went into a spin. Svendsen recovered control of the plane and the crew were told to use their parachutes. The navigator, Pilot Officer Irvin, failed to get out. His body was found in the wreckage of the aircraft.

The operations report for the mission states: 'Weather good. Small amount of low cloud increasing after 4.30 a.m. Ten aircraft detailed to attack Dusseldorf. Nine aircraft attacked target successfully. One failed to return (F/Lt Svendsen).'

Svendsen was captured in the town of Düren, between Aachen and Cologne, and was taken to Dulag Luft, the transit camp near Frankfurt used by the Luftwaffe to interrogate captured Allied aircrew. He spent the rest of the war at camps in Germany and

Poland – but he would prove to be a restless prisoner bent on trying to regain his freedom.

While at Spangenberg Castle in Hesse, Svendsen tried to escape with four other airmen, including Pilot Officer Allan McSweyn of the Royal Australian Air Force. According to the historian Charles Rollings, the author of *Wire and Walls: RAF Prisoners of War in Itzehoe, Spangenberg and Thorn 1939–42*, their plan required a stormy night to keep the sentries in their shelters.

'When a suitable night finally presented itself, the escapers were ready. With utmost stealth they made their way to an unoccupied room with their camp-made rope and grappling hook. At an opportune moment, Svendsen hurled the hook out towards the drawbridge. It did not engage, so he quickly hauled it in and hurled it out again. He began to pull the rope in a second time, and the hook snagged and held.

'As the senior member of the group, Svendsen had elected to go across first . . . [he] started off on his short but hazardous journey along the wet and slippery rope, hand over hand in the cold, driving rain. Then, just as he was in reach of the drawbridge, a bored guard, who had been sheltering in the sentry box, strolled out and stared idly at the moat. To his astonishment he saw Svendsen dangling from the length of the rope below him, and raised the alarm.'

McSweyn got back to his bed in the castle without being arrested, but Svendsen was given seven days' solitary confinement. He later succeeded in escaping from the punishment cells at Oflag VIB at Warburg and was outside the wire for three days before being arrested by the Gestapo. He was involved in the digging of several tunnels, including the most famous of them all, 'Tom', 'Dick' and 'Harry', which were constructed for the Great Escape from North Compound at Stalag Luft III at Sagan in Silesia.

Seventy-six men broke out of the camp through 'Harry', but most were recaptured and fifty of them were shot by the Germans in retaliation. Svendsen was one of the 200 men waiting in Hut 105 that night to enter the tunnel, but it was discovered before the New Zealander got his chance.

At much the same time, he was pursued by the RAF about a car he had left at Scampton – a Morris 8HP. According to an extraordinary letter from the Air Ministry, sent to Stalag Luft III, the under-secretary of state was urgently seeking instructions for disposal of the vehicle.

Svendsen was liberated in May 1945, almost four years after being shot down. As well as the DFC, he was awarded a chestful of campaign medals: the 1939–45 Star, the Air Crew Europe Star, the Defence Medal, War Medal 1939–45, and the Bomber Command Medal, Prisoner of War. And in addition to the Goldfish Club, he became a member of the Caterpillar Club, whose membership is open only to those who have successfully used a parachute to escape from a disabled aircraft. When the war ended, Svendsen returned to 9 Squadron flying Lancaster bombers. He was part of the crew that went to India for the independence celebrations in 1946, performing fly-pasts for the vice-regal party.

According to his family, he would have liked to have remained in the RAF, but the service was cutting back and he saw fewer opportunities for a career. His promotion to squadron leader was listed in the *London Gazette* on 18 November 1947, several months after he had left the service and returned to New Zealand. His brothers Fred and Gordon also flew during the war and lived to return home.

He then rejoined the family's dairy business in Pukekohe and, working with his father and three brothers, built up a modern treatment station that supplied milk to the local area until the 1980s, when it was sold to a big co-operative.

In 1950, three years after returning to the southern hemisphere, Svendsen married Ella Lorraine Vickers, whom he had met when he delivered milk to the business where she worked as a secretary. The couple had two children: a daughter Lynne, who visited Stalag Luft III in 1996, more than fifty-one years after her father had helped to build those famous tunnels, and a son, Christian.

Svendsen was active with veterans' associations, including the New Zealand ex-Prisoner of War Association, and joined reunions in Britain, Australia and Canada. He liked a game of bowls and never lost his love of flying. He joined the local Ardmore Aero Club and, for many years, he enjoyed 'joy-riding' as he put it, flying a Cessna 150, free from the dangers of flak and enemy fighters, over Franklin County, south of Auckland.

The Handley Page Hampden did not survive the war. It was

withdrawn from front-line duties with Bomber Command in 1942, and then served with Coastal Command as a torpedo bomber for a further year. Of the approximately 1,500 aircraft built, 714 were lost on operations, and 263 in various crashes; 1,077 crew were killed with a further 739 listed as missing.

Neil Svendsen lived for sixty-two years after being shot down in 1941 on his last wartime mission. He died on 14 March 2003, aged eighty-eight, after suffering a stroke – a former dairy farmer, born and bred thousands of miles from the battlefields where his skill and courage had an impact on the course of the Second World War.

The rusted and battered wreck of the Dornier 17 bomber believed to have been flown by Willi Effmert was lifted from the sea floor off the coast of Kent in 2013, 73 years after it was shot down

10

Flight Sergeant Willi Effmert
Dornier 17 Medium Bomber

26 August 1940

If he had kept that plane up for another three minutes,
he would have made the shoreline.

O N A CLEAR and sunny day, if you look up almost anywhere
in south-east England, you can see the front line of the Battle
of Britain; close your eyes and perhaps you can imagine the German
bombers, their engines humming high above.

On one such morning, nearly eighty years after the battle, Dave
Lawrence headed out to sea off the attractive coastal town of Deal
in south-east Kent, to help research one of those aircraft. The
Dornier 17 medium bomber, which is believed to have been flown
by Willi Effmert and his crew, ditched in the sea on 26 August 1940.

As Lawrence made his way offshore to the plane's last resting place,
the easternmost ramparts of the white cliffs of Dover were clearly
visible in the haze behind him. Above him, high in the sky where
Effmert was shot down by an RAF Boulton Paul Defiant, passenger
jets flying to the capitals of twenty-first-century Europe carved out
vapour trails on the old aerial hunting grounds of the Battle of Britain.

At the wheel of his small blue-hulled fishing boat, the *Gary Ann*,
Lawrence, aged sixty-five, recalled seeing the rusted and battered
German bomber on the day it was lifted from the sea floor in June
2013. It had been lying there for seventy-three years. The last licensed
fisherman working off the steep shingle beach at Deal, Lawrence
is a stocky figure in a battle-hardened, blue smock top, with a
weather-beaten face fringed by heavy sideboards and topped off
with a flat skipper's cap.

Lawrence was fishing nearby when the only surviving 'Flying Pencil' in the world was slowly and precariously winched on to a salvage barge. 'The fuselage was very, very thin, so they were lucky to get it up in one piece,' he said, recalling the lift operation near the Goodwin Fork buoy.

He had often thought about what must have been going through the mind of the twenty-four-year-old German, as he attempted to crash-land his stricken plane on Goodwin Sands at low water. It was a risky manoeuvre born out of desperation and it almost certainly ended with the aircraft somersaulting into water that was about 50ft deep.

The area of sand Effmert was aiming for is exposed for a couple of hours through each cycle of the spring tide and lies about five nautical miles off Deal seafront, but it hardly counts as an emergency runway.

'He was probably coming across and saw the sandbank and tried to touch down on it, but overshot and that's where he finished up,' said Lawrence, pointing at an area of water about half a mile inshore of the sandbank. 'They would have had lifejackets on and, in them days, a lot of the local boats were on the lookout for anyone in trouble.'

As he surveyed the tranquil scene, with seals in the distance basking in the sunshine on the exposed banks, Lawrence reflected on how close the young pilot was to coming down on terra firma. A hard landing had its own risks, but it might have saved the lives of two of his three crew members who died after the Dornier ditched.

'If he had kept that plane up for another three or four minutes, he would have made the shoreline or a safe landing on Sandwich Bay,' explained Lawrence. 'Where they did end up, it would have sunk within minutes. In them days, it would have been sand there and the weight of the aircraft would have buried it in the sand.'

The day that Effmert climbed aboard his Dornier 17 for the last time at an airfield at St Trond in Belgium was one of the busiest of the entire Battle of Britain; waves of German bombers escorted by large numbers of fighters attacked airfields and other targets in southern England.

In the morning, German aircraft, including the Do 17 flown by

Effmert, bombed Folkestone, Dover, Margate and Broadstairs and the RAF fighter stations of Kenley and Biggin Hill, near London. Later they hit Plymouth, Portsmouth and Southampton, with its big Supermarine factory making Spitfires. That night Coventry and Birmingham, home to large engineering works for the aircraft industry, were also targeted.

In London, Churchill entertained Geoffrey Dawson, the editor of *The Times*, to lunch at Downing Street. Dawson reported that the prime minister was in 'excellent form, fit and confident'. According to Martin Gilbert, Churchill's biographer, the air raid sirens sounded as lunch ended. It was the first of the expected retaliation raids after the British attack on Berlin twelve hours earlier.

'Churchill at once ordered guests and staff to the shelters,' wrote Gilbert. 'On learning that the next British bomber target was Leipzig, and not Berlin, he minuted to the Chief of the Air Staff: "Now that they have begun to molest the capital, I want you to hit them hard, and Berlin is the place to hit them."'

The Luftwaffe may, as Churchill put it, have been 'molesting' London in the wake of the RAF's raid on Berlin, but Hitler and Goering had yet to make the momentous decision to bomb British cities indiscriminately. At that moment, the outlook for Air Chief Marshal Sir Hugh Dowding and his fighter force still looked bleak and it was the defence of the British airfields that was regarded as the critical issue.

Britain's seemingly precarious position was noted farther afield. That day the American news magazine *Time* carried a portrait of Field Marshal Erhard Milch on its cover. Milch had overseen the development of German aircraft production in the build-up to the war. Inside it ran an article headlined: 'Great Britain: War Nerves'. Another article, entitled 'Western Theatre: Assault in the Air', described the latest combat in the Battle of Britain. 'There has never before been an air battle such as was fought last week in the sky over Britain,' it reported.

The travails of war were not the sole preserve of the British, though. On 26 August, there was also an attack in Ireland by two German bombers, violating Dublin's neutrality. Three women were killed when four bombs were dropped on the Shelburne Agricultural Co-operative Society creamery in the village of

Campile, County Wexford. It appears that the German aircrew mistook Campile for targets in south Wales. The government of Eamon de Valera issued an official complaint that prompted a Nazi apology three days later.

Back over southern England, however, British RAF pilots found that they were not alone as they fought to protect the south coast from the threat of invasion. The Czech airmen of 310 Squadron distinguished themselves in the latest rounds of aerial combat and 1 Squadron of the Royal Canadian Air Force entered the battle, the first Canadian unit to confront the enemy. While imminent decisions in Berlin would ease the pressure on RAF Command, there were also one or two helpful straws in the wind elsewhere that would aid Britain's cause.

Under Felix Eboue, the first black governor to rule a French overseas territory, Chad became the first colony to join the Allies and reject the embrace of collaborators in Vichy France. Closer to home, Hitler transferred twelve army divisions, including two armoured divisions, from France to Poland, in what appears to have been the first signal that he was abandoning hope of invading England and was instead turning his attention towards expansion eastwards.

The plane flown by Effmert on that day – the Dornier 17 – had been developed in 1932, before the advent of the Third Reich, supposedly as a high-speed transport for passengers and mail; its real purpose was as a light bomber and reconnaissance aircraft that was intended to be fast and agile and capable of outrunning fighters.

The Flying Pencil, so-called because of its thin fuselage, was designed and built by Claudius Dornier at the factories of Dornier Flugzeugwerke in Friedrichshafen. A prototype first flew in November 1934. It became one of the three main Luftwaffe bombers deployed during the first three years of war and it played a central role in the Battle of Britain.

The Do 17 featured twin Bramo engines mounted on a 'shoulder wing' structure and innovative self-sealing fuel tanks embedded in its fuselage and wings. It could fly at 220 mph and carry bombs weighing 2,200lb for a distance of 210 miles. The Dornier carried a crew of four – a pilot, bombardier and two gunners – in the forward section of the fuselage, with its protruding

Dornier crews studying their maps at bases in France and on their way to targets in England

and clear glass canopy. Later variants of the plane carried up to eight machine guns.

During its development, the Do 17 – which looks rather like a giant dragonfly – was regarded as an advanced aircraft that was quicker than almost all single-seat fighters of the time. It was initially popular with German bomber crews, because it handled well at low altitude and its slender structure was thought to make it hard to hit.

The Do 17 first entered active service during the Spanish Civil War. It then held the distinction of carrying out the first aerial combat mission of the Second World War, when a Do 17 took off from Heiligenbeil in east Prussia and bombed the approaches to a rail bridge at Dirschau in north-west Poland.

The aircraft played a key role in attacks on Allied shipping in July 1940 and, alongside the Heinkel 111, was used intensively in the Battle of Britain. Here its shortcomings in defensive armament and lack of armoured protection for its crews became increasingly evident.

The Do 17 was used in all areas of the German war effort until the end of 1941, when its limited bomb load and flying range made way for the Junkers 88. In all, 2,139 Do 17s were built and they were also used by the air forces of Yugoslavia, Spain and Finland.

Effmert and his crew were part of a group of twelve Dornier 17s sent out from Belgium to attack the RAF airfields at Debden and Hornchurch in Essex. They were also expected to lure and distract British fighters, who then found themselves overwhelmed by a large formation of Messerschmitt Bf 109s that were following the bombers across the North Sea.

The fact that 26 August was a fine, clear day and excellent for flying was undeniable, but the planes with the swastikas on their tailfins were easy to spot. The RAF's early warning systems picked up the Dorniers well out to sea and the Defiants of 264 Squadron were scrambled from Hornchurch to intercept them.

In his memoirs, Desmond Hughes, who would go on to become an Air Vice-Marshal, recalled flying as a pilot officer alongside Air Gunner Sergeant Fred Gash and seeing the bombers in the distance at 11,000ft. 'The specks grew into pencil-slim silhouettes of Dornier

17s and suddenly there were black crosses insolently challenging us in our own backyard,' he wrote.

The Defiants climbed up to attack the bombers over Herne Bay and Deal and while they did so, they found themselves being 'harassed', according to the Intelligence Combat Report for 264 Squadron that day, 'by at least fifty Bf 109s which kept diving on them and appeared to be otherwise unengaged'.

Hughes and Gash claimed two Do 17s were destroyed in an engagement in which six of the German bombers and one Bf 109 were reported shot down; three Defiants were also lost. It is not known if Hughes's tally included Effmert's plane, although some researchers believe it did.

Describing his first kill, Hughes wrote: 'Fred Gash took as his target the second Dornier and made no mistake. His De Wilde incendiaries twinkled all over it, but particularly its engine. It began to fall out of formation, the hatch was jettisoned, two parachutes streamed out, as little dark figures bailed out, and the stricken aircraft went down increasingly steeply with its starboard engine well alight.'

It is thought that Effmert's plane was attacked after it fell out of formation and he and his crew lost their bearings while flying through cloud. The plane was hit in both engines and in the cockpit, where Effmert shared the cramped space with Sergeant Hermann Ritzel, aged twenty-one, from Frankfurt am Main, Sergeant Helmut Reinhardt, aged twenty-seven, from Bochum, and Corporal Heinz Huhn, aged twenty-one, from Lotterfeld.

Ritzel lost two fingers on his left hand as a result of incoming fire and it is thought one of the engines stopped, forcing Effmert to try to land on the Goodwin Sands below him. After the plane hit the water with its wheels up, Effmert and Ritzel managed to get out and were captured and taken prisoner. Both Reinhardt and Huhn died, either from wounds sustained in the air, the impact of the crash-landing, or from drowning. Reinhardt's body was washed ashore in the Netherlands some days later. He was buried at the large German cemetery at Ysselsteyn in the Netherlands, while Huhn was interred in the German war cemetery at Cannock Chase in Staffordshire.

Effmert and Ritzel were held in Britain before being shipped as prisoners of war to Canada, where they spent the remainder of the conflict. When Effmert eventually returned home to Bad Salzuflen, near Hanover, he found that his wife had been killed in an Allied air raid. It is thought that he remarried several years later and died in the late 1990s.

Ritzel married after the war and had a daughter, before divorcing and marrying for a second time. He worked as an engineer at Fulda, north-east of Frankfurt, and died in 1996. His grandson, Christian Nowak, told the *Daily Telegraph* in 2013 that his grandfather had not been a member of the Nazi party before the war and had joined the Luftwaffe because he had experience flying gliders.

'He had a normal life. He liked to go hiking in the Alps. He liked to draw pictures and he spent a lot of time in his garden. He never flew again. I think he was unable to fly a glider because of the injury to his hand,' he said. 'After the war he was an absolute opponent of war. But at the time, in an air battle, it's you or him. And you have to save your own life. The goal is to survive.'

Nowak said he did not think of his grandfather with pride because of his wartime experience, but because he was an engineer, who discovered some advances in electronics that he patented. 'I am proud of him for that,' he said.

The operation to raise Effmert's plane took place thirteen years after a fisherman fouled his nets on the wreck. The aircraft was found lying upside down with its bomb doors open. It was first surveyed in 2008 by Wessex Archaeology on behalf of English Heritage. Subsequent surveys confirmed that considerable parts of the tail section were missing and that recreational or 'sports' divers had removed some artefacts, including two machine guns, although four others remained with the wreck.

After completing a big fundraising drive, the Royal Air Force Museum announced that the wreck would be recovered in May 2013. The Ministry of Defence (MoD) authorised the salvage operation after deciding that the shell of the plane did not constitute a war grave since all the crew had been accounted for and no human remains were present. When the operation to lift the aircraft began, the salvage was hampered by bad weather and escalating costs, but the plane was finally raised clear of the water on 10 June 2013 and taken to the RAF Museum at Cosford in Shropshire.

Once it arrived there, it was placed in a polytunnel for twenty months, while it was sprayed around the clock with citric acid to stabilise the metal and neutralise impurities from salt water. After that it was covered by tarpaulins and subjected to continuous drying using dehumidifiers for more than a year. Once the restoration work has been completed, the museum intends to put the Dornier on public display.

In the course of their work, the experts at Cosford discovered that the plane did not go up in flames at any stage before it crashed and that it was hit by both shrapnel and machine gun bullets, suggesting that it was damaged by ground fire before it was finished off by the Defiants.

Back on the water off Deal, Lawrence marvelled at Effmert's skill in getting his aircraft down on, or close to, a strip of sand that remains as treacherous now as it has been for hundreds of years.

'The Goodwin is a really eerie place and when you are on it, you have water all around you and you know the tide is going to come up – it's not a nice place to be,' he said. 'The sands are quite wide, but I don't think it would have been wide enough for a runway. As he was crash-landing, he wouldn't have been too worried as long as he could get out of it when they hit the water.'

A portrait of Franz von Werra, who flew the Messerschmitt Bf 109,
which was the perfect plane for a self-confident, swashbuckling fighter pilot.
He was embraced by the Nazi propaganda machine

II

First Lieutenant Baron Franz von Werra
Messerschmitt Bf 109E Single-Engine Fighter

5 September 1940

He was good-looking, arrogant and not averse
to portraying himself in a heroic light.

UNFORTUNATELY FOR FIGHTER Command, 5 September
provided perfect conditions for aerial combat; the Allied
leaders had been praying for low-level clouds and rain to give
Britain's defences and its exhausted pilots a breathing space from
the relentless onslaught by the Luftwaffe.

High in the sky over London, German bombers and fighter
escorts were making their way up the Thames estuary in formation.
Their target was Biggin Hill aerodrome and their attack was preceded
by a diversionary move against Croydon airfield that the Luftwaffe
hoped would entice RAF fighters away from Biggin Hill. The ruse
did not work, however, and fighters from 79 Squadron attacked the
bombers as they approached Biggin Hill, as a result of which many
of the German munitions fell wide of the mark.

Among the German aircraft flying home from Kent was a
Messerschmitt Bf 109 flown by Baron Franz von Werra – one of
thirty fighter escorts for the bombers. It was the start of a great
odyssey for the Swiss pilot.

Alongside the Hawker Hurricane and the Supermarine Spitfire
on the Allied side, the Messerschmitt Bf 109 is the most widely
known of the aircraft that took part in the Battle of Britain, reflecting
its key role for the Luftwaffe as a fighter escort for German bombers
trying to destroy Britain's airfields, aircraft and cities.

The Bf 109 was the Luftwaffe's only single-engine fighter and it was a remarkably successful flying machine, becoming the most prolific attack aircraft in history, with 33,984 airframes built between 1936 and April 1945. In some conditions the Messerschmitt could outmanoeuvre not only the Hurricane but also the Spitfire, and its pilots were responsible for the majority of the 1,172 aircraft lost by RAF Fighter Command between July and October 1940. Over the same period 610 of the German planes were lost.

Like the Spitfire, the Messerschmitt was based on a finely designed, all-metal monocoque with only the movable control surfaces and flaps covered by fabric. Powered by a V12 aero engine, it was fast, agile and armed with a combination of cannon and machine guns that could destroy Hurricanes and Spitfires with two short bursts of fire at close range.

One big advantage that it held over its British-built equivalents was its direct fuel injection engine. This meant that its pilots could dive from level flight without any interruption to the fuel supply caused by negative gravitational force. By contrast the Spitfire's carburettor engine would momentarily stop in a steep dive, losing its pilots precious seconds in a dogfight.

Adolf Galland, one of the most famous aces who flew the Bf 109 throughout the Battle of Britain, amassing fifty-seven kills by the end of 1940, remarked on this in his 1953 memoir, *The First and the Last.* 'The British fighters usually tried to shake off pursuit by a half-roll or a half-roll on top of a loop,' he recalled, 'while we simply went straight for them, with wide-open throttle and eyes bulging out of our sockets.'

While the Messerschmitt could also climb higher than a Spitfire, which gave German pilots more freedom to escape or re-engage in a dogfight, the plane had its disadvantages, as assessments of captured planes by the RAF showed during the war.

A cramped cockpit, for example, affected the ability of the pilot to exert force on the control column. The German fighter was also a notoriously tricky aircraft to land, with its canted undercarriage often causing it to spin round. On a hard landing, the relatively lightweight undercarriage could collapse, an Achilles heel that, in 1939 alone, contributed to 255 landing accidents.

Designed in 1933 by Professor Wilhelm 'Willy' Messerschmitt and Robert Lusser, in response to a design brief issued by the

German aviation ministry for a single-engine fighter that could reach speeds of 250 mph and an altitude of 19,500ft, the Bf 109 was armed with two machine guns or one cannon; it needed to be a highly manoeuvrable and versatile plane to replace the obsolete Heinkel and Arado biplanes.

The prototype first flew in May 1935 with a Rolls-Royce Kestrel engine, supplied by the British factory as part of a four-engine deal in exchange for a Heinkel 70, which was used as an engine test bed.

The Messerschmitt easily outperformed its rival prototypes, manufactured by Focke-Wulf, Arado and Heinkel, and it made its first public flight at the Berlin Olympics in 1936. A year later a Bf 109 flown by the company's chief pilot, Dr Hermann Wurster, set a new world air-speed record for landplanes with piston engines of 379.62 mph.

First used in combat in the Spanish Civil War, the Bf 109 played an important role in all the early phases of the Second World War, including the invasion of Poland and the Battle of France. After the Battle of Britain, it continued to be a mainstay of the Luftwaffe's offensive operations alongside a new German fighter, the Focke-Wulf 190. The Messerschmitt played a prominent role in the conquest of Yugoslavia and the invasion of the Soviet Union and it was responsible for more kills than any other aircraft flying during the Second World War.

Adolf Galland paid this tribute to an impressive example of German design and ingenuity which, at the start of the Battle of Britain, he believed was superior to the Spitfire. 'The Me [Bf] 109 was at the time the best fighter plane in the world,' he wrote, eight years after the end of the war. 'It was not only superior to all enemy types between 1935 and 1940, but was also a pioneer and prototype for international fighter construction.

'The Me 109 did not result from demands made by aerial warfare. On the contrary, it was a gift from the ingenious designer Messerschmitt, which was at first looked upon with great distrust and was nearly turned down altogether. It was put into mass production far too late. Had this stage been reached during the first two years of the war, it would have given the Germans absolute supremacy in the air.'

It was, in other words, the perfect machine for a self-confident and swashbuckling fighter pilot such as Franz von Werra. He was good-looking, daring, arrogant and not averse to embellishing the stories of his derring-do in his Bf 109 to portray himself in a heroic light.

He was christened François Gustave de Werra and was born in July 1914 in Leuk, in the Valais region of Switzerland, to an old ennobled family.

Shortly after his birth, however, his father was financially ruined and the young de Werra and his sister were taken in by a family friend, Baroness Luisa van Haber, who lived at Beuron in southern Germany. She and her husband had no children and de Werra came to regard them as his parents, cutting off all contact with his mother and father. He also changed his name from François to Franz and from de Werra to von Werra.

His foster-mother, who went on to divorce her husband, was a tough disciplinarian and life was not always happy for the young von Werra. In his early teens, he ran away from home and lived rough in Hamburg for a few days, before managing to land a job as a cabin boy with the Hamburg–Amerika Line. He then sailed to New Orleans. Although he was eventually shipped back home, the trip to America gave the young man his first taste of adventure, and he loved the attention he received when he returned to school as a hero.

After school, in the years that followed the Great Depression, von Werra worked as a gardener and then as a locksmith's mate until the Nazis came to power. He later volunteered for the newly formed German Air Force as a private. After two years of basic training, he was selected for flying training. It was while he was making his way in the new Luftwaffe that he decided to adopt his original family's ancient title *Freiherr* – or baron. This was part of his plan to get himself noticed, which also included stunts such as flying under bridges, performing aerobatics over his girlfriend's home, and being towed behind a sports car across an airfield in a bathtub.

The young Baron von Werra was a cocky, forceful character and some of his superiors found him too much to take, although others could see his potential. 'He is the fighter type,' one of them is quoted as saying in James Leasor and Kendal Burt's account of von

Werra's life, *The One That Got Away*. '[He is] extremely dashing, good-looking and humorous. Absolutely reliable. Some of his pranks misfire, but it is impossible to be mad with him. He would cut off his arm for his commanding officer.'

Having survived one bad crash in training in a Bf 109, von Werra was in a hurry to become a national hero. By 5 September, he was credited with four kills in the Battle of Britain – three Hurricanes and a Spitfire – but he also claimed to have destroyed five more planes in an episode a few days earlier. The British were confident, however, that no such event had taken place.

Von Werra claimed to have been involved in a dogfight over London in which he shot down a Spitfire, but in the course of the exchange, his radio had been damaged and he had become separated from the rest of his formation. It was while hedge-hopping back along the Thames towards the North Sea that he claimed to have come across RAF fighters circling as they prepared to land at an unidentified airfield.

In an episode that was reported in detail in the *Berliner Zeitung* newspaper on 28 August under the headline, 'German Fighter Pilot's Daring Exploit Over England', and which earned him a much-coveted Knight's Cross, von Werra described how he decided to join the RAF planes and make it look as if he was one of them by lowering his undercarriage and beginning an approach.

Then, after retracting his undercarriage and opening the throttle on his Messerschmitt, he shot down the last of the approaching British planes and proceeded to destroy three more on the ground, which caught fire after a petrol tanker exploded. For good measure, he followed up with more low-level attacks in the face of fierce anti-aircraft resistance from the ground, and destroyed one more plane before making good his escape.

Whatever the truth was, the story helped to create a reputation for von Werra in Germany as one of Goering's most successful pilots and he made the most of the attention he received from the Nazi propaganda machine.

In the days before he was shot down, von Werra had been photographed by a popular German radio magazine leaning against the wing of his Messerschmitt, holding his pet lion cub in his arms at the airfield in the Pas de Calais where he was based. The caption reads: 'This is the *Staffel* [squadron] lion, Simba, taking the place of the British Lion, who seldom shows himself in the vicinity of German fighter pilots!'

A few weeks earlier, during the lull in fighting between the fall of France and the start of the Battle of Britain, von Werra and another pilot had spent an afternoon in their Messerschmitts buzzing cars on the roads near their airfield. One of their 'victims' was a colonel riding in the back of a solitary German staff car, who was subjected to one low-level mock attack after another, which he did not enjoy at all. He took down von Werra's markings and filed a report that precipitated court martial proceedings.

However, the events of 5 September put that case on hold for good. As von Werra was making his way east towards the North Sea, 6,000ft above the formation of bombers he was helping to protect, six Spitfires of 41 Squadron appeared above and behind him. Seconds after the pilot of the last Messerschmitt in the group had warned of the presence of enemy fighters on the radio, three Spitfires dived almost vertically through the fighter screen to attack the bombers below.

Immediately in front of von Werra, his commanding officer, Hauptmann Erich von Selle, dived to chase the British planes and von Werra followed. As he did so, another Spitfire behind him opened fire, almost certainly aiming at von Selle, but it was von Werra's plane that took the hits.

The pilot who liked to be known as the 'Terror of the British Airforce' rolled his plane and dived steeply, trying to evade the fighter on his tail. But von Werra quickly realised that his engine was dying as it overheated, forcing him to look for a suitable place to crash-land.

He came down in a recently harvested cornfield with the Messerschmitt – its wheels up – coming to rest in a cloud of dust. A few seconds later, the Swiss pilot opened the hinged glass canopy over his cockpit and, having pulled off his leather helmet, jumped off a wing on to the ground and stood casually looking at his stricken plane.

When he noticed soldiers approaching from a nearby searchlight battery, von Werra quickly removed documents from his breast pocket and, using his lighter, set fire to them as the soldiers ran

Von Werra with his pet lion cub, Simba, in France, and the wreckage of his fighter in an English field

towards him. The first man to reach him was the unarmed battery cook and soon von Werra – whose identity papers were now in cinders on the ground – was being marched off under guard as the fighting continued in the skies above him.

Von Werra had no plans to spend the rest of his war as a captive and he proved a resourceful and determined escaper. Having been interviewed and processed, he was sent to a prisoner-of-war camp for German officers at Grizedale Hall in the Lake District, from where he promptly escaped during an exercise march through the countryside. He was found after a massive search operation, during which he had spent six days trying to make his way to the Irish Sea in dismal autumnal weather.

He was then moved to another prison camp near Derby where, ever resourceful, he organised a successful tunnelling operation. Once out of captivity for a second time, he tried to steal a Hurricane from a nearby airfield, while pretending to be a Dutch airman who had crash-landed after his bomber was hit over Denmark. It was a typically audacious plan and von Werra came close to pulling it off, but he was rearrested as he sat in the cockpit of the British fighter, trying to work out how to fly the machine.

Along with thousands of other German prisoners, von Werra was then shipped to Canada, where he succeeded in escaping for a third time, on this occasion from a train transporting him and thousands of other prisoners from the docks to a PoW camp. He managed to get across the partially frozen St Lawrence River – an extremely perilous endeavour – before enjoying himself for several months in New York, at a time when the United States was neutral.

But having made his mark in the Battle of Britain, the urge to fly again for the Luftwaffe was overwhelming and von Werra left the United States illegally and made his way to Italy and finally Germany by way of Mexico, Panama, Peru and Brazil.

He arrived in Berlin in April 1941 and was summoned to the Reich Chancellery, where he received his Knight's Cross from Hitler in person. Von Werra then spent several weeks helping German intelligence agencies and offering advice on how German prisoners should deal with British interrogation techniques.

It was after testing a Messerschmitt for the first time since he had been shot down, at the Werneuchen Fighter School in mid-June, that von Werra finally got his wish to return to front-line combat and was posted to command a fighter squadron. He spent a short spell on the eastern front, where he was officially credited with eight more victories, before his unit was moved to the Netherlands, where it was equipped with the new F-4 variant of the Messerschmitt.

At that stage, twenty-seven-year-old von Werra had just got married, having packed an enormous amount into his life. Yet it was to come to an abrupt end. On the morning of 25 October, he led a patrol of three fighters, dipping his wings over the cottage he shared with his wife before heading out to sea.

About twenty miles offshore, von Werra's plane developed an engine fault and before the other two pilots accompanying him realised anything was wrong, his aircraft had plummeted into the North Sea. All rescue efforts proved fruitless – no trace of von Werra or his Messerschmitt were ever found.

The dashing Canadian Keith 'Skeets' Ogilvie in front of a Spitfire. His life was an epic story: he played American football, was a fighter ace, and broke out of Stalag Luft III during the Great Escape

12

Pilot Officer Keith Ogilvie
Supermarine Spitfire Mk I Single-Engine Fighter

7 September 1940

*My insides were frozen and my heart was
beating up where my tonsils should be.*

ON THE MORNING of 7 September, Pilot Officer Keith Ogilvie – a charismatic young Canadian itching to get involved in the action after months of training – was lounging around with his fellow pilots in 609 Squadron at Middle Wallop airfield in Hampshire.

Sitting in the dispersal hut only yards from his Spitfire, twenty-four-year-old Ogilvie, who was nicknamed 'Skeets' for his prowess as a running back in American football, was on standby on one of the most glorious mornings of the entire summer. The temperature was about 70°F (21°C) and the skies were almost entirely clear.

What Ogilvie and his fellow pilots did not know, as they waited for the Operations phone to ring, was that this was the day when Hitler and Goering switched from attacking the RAF and its airfields to focus on bombing London. Although British civilians were about to suffer greatly as the Blitz began, the RAF was able to regroup and recover in what is regarded by historians as a turning point in the battle in favour of Britain; the threat of invasion was suddenly receding.

So enraged was the German dictator by the raids on Berlin in the past few days that he authorised wholesale attacks on London.

In the two weeks leading up to this moment, the Luftwaffe had retained the upper hand. Fighter Command had endured the deaths of 103 pilots, with a further 128 seriously wounded – accounting for about a quarter of its pilots. In addition, 466 Spitfires and Hurricanes had been destroyed or seriously damaged.

Reflecting on these events twenty years later, Air Vice-Marshal Keith Park, who was Air Chief Marshal Sir Hugh Dowding's right-hand man and the commander of 11 Group in south-east England, said: 'Had Goering carried on for another week or ten days hammering my fighter airfields, he might have had them out of action and we could have lost the battle.'

Churchill also believed this was a key moment. In *The Second World War, Volume II: Their Finest Hour*, he described the airfields as having been 'terribly knocked about', and said the switch by the Germans 'gave us a breathing space of which we had the utmost need'.

He wrote: 'It was therefore with a sense of relief that Fighter Command felt the German attack turn on to London on 7 September, and concluded that the enemy had changed its plan. Goering should certainly have persevered against the airfields . . . he made a foolish mistake.'

The Germans changed their focus with massive force in what they called Operation London. On that beautiful Saturday morning, Goering sent hundreds of planes across the Channel with 348 bombers in the first wave alone, escorted by 617 fighters, the most forbidding force arrayed against Britain since the Spanish Armada. As one Spitfire pilot recalled: 'There were so many enemy fighters layered up to 30,000ft that it was just like looking up the escalator at Piccadilly Circus.'

Goering took personal command of the attack. He had arrived on the French coast the previous day and watched from the cliffs of Cap Gris-Nez in the Pas de Calais as the German aircraft headed for the English coast. 'They flew at a very great height, glistening like beautiful steel birds in the afternoon sunshine,' recalled the American journalist Ben Robertson.

The altitude chosen by the Luftwaffe caused new problems for the RAF and the anti-aircraft gunners on the ground. British radar struggled to identify planes flying at greater heights and pilots such as Skeets Ogilvie had to climb farther to engage their German counterparts. It was also much harder for the RAF pilots to get above the Luftwaffe formation to press home an attack in the most advantageous way.

The first wave of bombers was followed that day by a second, 300-strong bomber fleet that attacked the Surrey Docks in east London, killing 436 people on the ground and injuring more than 1,600. This came to be regarded as the start of the Blitz; the German bombers would return on many nights throughout the next eight months.

Desmond Flower witnessed the destruction near the docks as he rode pillion on a motorbike on his way home through south London. 'The columns of smoke merged and became a monstrous curtain that blocked the sky,' he wrote. 'Only the billows within it and the sudden shafts of flame which shot up hundreds of feet made one realise that it was a living thing and not just the backdrop of some nightmare opera.'

At Middle Wallop, the bell for action stations rang at 1.00 p.m. as Ogilvie and his fellow pilots ran for their Spitfires. The orders were 'London' and '20,000ft'. By the time the Canadian was in his seat in the most famous British fighter of them all, the ground crews were there, strapping him in and rushing to pull the chocks away from the wheels. With his Merlin engine ticking over, he taxied for take-off, ready to see action for the first time.

One of three sons of a railway engineer from Ottawa, Ogilvie had volunteered for the RAF just over a year before. When the Royal Canadian Air Force (RCAF) turned him down because he did not have a degree, he crossed the street to the RAF recruiting office and signed up. Within a few days, he was on a ship from Canada to England where his training began.

The young Canadian, who at one stage had been invited to play for the Ottawa Rough Riders professional football team, was mad about flying and had eagerly followed the exploits of the pioneering aviator Charles Lindbergh. When he arrived in England, he was attached to the De Havilland School of Flying in Hatfield, in Hertfordshire, where he discovered that English beer was not to his liking, describing it as a 'cruel disappointment'.

It was from Hatfield that he went solo for the first time. 'The thrill was unlike any other I have experienced,' he recalled. 'On the first circuit I bounced her and scurried across the 'drome like a startled deer. The second landing was no hell, but at least I got it down. Today I am a pilot.'

Ogilvie was doing what he wanted – making a contribution at a time of peril – and loving every minute in the air and on the ground. In September 1939, he flew his first loop in a Tiger Moth and later that month he crash-landed in a field of hay when his engine cut out while he was doing aerobatics.

After narrowly avoiding being sidelined – as he saw it – into an instructing role, he began fighter training at Aston Down in Gloucestershire in July 1940. It was here that he made his debut in a Spitfire.

It was an experience the ebullient young Ogilvie would never forget. 'I got into this thing and opened it up, and just rocketed into the sky [and I] hardly knew what was going on,' he recalled. During that first fifty-minute flight he couldn't get the canopy to close and had to hold it with one hand throughout, but he still managed to land the plane safely.

In a letter to his family in Ottawa, quoted in *You Never Know Your Luck*, the biography written by his son Keith, Skeets Ogilvie described the 'business of coping' with the Spitfire, remarking that the terrific speed no longer scared him to death. 'The first few days, I don't mind admitting, [were] a little shaking but I have the swing of it now . . . what ships!' he wrote.

He explained exactly what a physical challenge the Spitfire was for its pilot. 'If you suddenly try to change your path of flight, everything goes blotto. The idea is just to stay within the blackout stage,' he wrote, adding: 'I never used to perspire, but when I get out of these babies I am absolutely soaking. Two hours a day in these thunder buggies and you are poohed right out.'

By late August, Ogilvie had joined 609 Squadron and had undergone ten days of practice and familiarisation flying before going operational from Middle Wallop. He flew for another twelve hours before the momentous events of 7 September.

As Ogilvie and his wing arrived over their designated sector that day, they were warned over the radio to expect 200 German aircraft coming straight at them. He remembered seeing what looked like a cloud of little black beetles crawling towards him as he was ordered to engage.

This was the moment all his training had prepared him for. In third place in the leading section, Ogilvie half-rolled his Spitfire and dived for a side-on attack on the German formation, pumping machine gun bullets into the belly of one bomber that had been hit by a Spitfire ahead of him.

Then, finding himself in the middle of the German formation and being targeted by rear gunners on the bombers who holed his wing and tail, the Canadian dived to escape. After bottoming out but desperate to have another go, he put his Spitfire into a steep climb and, as he came back up, saw the bombers turning tail for home. At the same time, he was stunned to see two Messerschmitt 109s drifting right into his path.

He wrote in his diary:

By sheer blind luck I was in the sun to them and they either did not see me or figured I was another escorting fighter. Had they come out the other side of me . . . but we don't think about that. I opened fire on the second one which had a big number 19 on a silver background, and connected as he rolled over and dove, turning on his back. I got very close and emptied my guns as he streamed glycol, then smoke and finally a sheet of flame. This was a 'certain' and, now out of ammunition, I streaked for home.

Isolated in his little cockpit, Ogilvie was buzzing with the excitement and the adrenaline rush of combat. 'I could feel nothing,' he remembered, 'except my insides were frozen and my heart was beating up where my tonsils should be.'

That day 609 Squadron destroyed six enemy aircraft with six more 'probables' and, as Ogilvie noted, there were likely to be many more 'carrying scars' as they headed back to the French coast. In return the squadron had no casualties, although one pilot had to land at Maidenhead after a bullet damaged his engine.

Overall, during daylight combat that day, the Luftwaffe lost forty-one aircraft – fourteen bombers, sixteen Bf 109s, seven Messerschmitt 110s and four reconnaissance planes. Fighter Command, meanwhile, lost twenty-three aircraft with six pilots killed and seven wounded.

Of all the Allied aircraft that took part in the Battle of Britain, the Spitfire flown by Ogilvie and his peers is by far the best known. Even though the Hurricane was responsible for downing more German aircraft, it is the Spitfire that still evokes an emotional response from the general public.

The Reginald Mitchell-designed single-seater fighter, with its distinctive elliptical wings, elegant fuselage and growling Merlin engine, will forever be associated with Britain's darkest hour in 1940. And the sight of one of the many surviving Spitfires in flight today can bring a lump to the throat of those who witness it.

The reasons for the Spitfire's popularity and emotional resonance are many. Its very name evokes imagery of fierce dragon-like resistance; its characteristics in flight are graceful, both visually and aurally, and perhaps most importantly, the Spitfire was adored by its pilots, Ogilvie among them. More manoeuvrable than the Hurricane, it was as fast as the Bf 109, it was well armed and it was tough, which made it an ideal 'weapon' in the dogfighting that came to characterise the Battle of Britain in the popular imagination.

'She was so smooth and held no surprises in any way,' said the American pilot Lee Gover. 'I often marvelled at how this plane could be so easy to fly and yet how it could be such an effective fighter, able to hold its own with any plane in the world.' Another American pilot, James Goodson, described flying the Spitfire as something instinctive. He said it was like 'pulling on a pair of tight jeans'.

As it evolved, the Spitfire became even better and more powerful. 'It took my breath away,' recalled Brian Kingcome of his first flight in a Spitfire Mk IX, introduced in 1942. 'It was exhilarating, a feeling I could never forget. I yearned for a chance to demonstrate this astonishing new tool to the Germans.'

Spitfire pilots quickly understood how their fighting machine became far more than just another aircraft. The test pilot Jeffrey Quill said of it: 'The little Spitfire somehow captured the imagination of the British people at a time of near despair, becoming a symbol of defiance and of victory in what seemed a desperate and almost hopeless situation.'

The origins of the Spitfire go back to the early 1920s, when Mitchell led a team at the Supermarine aviation company in Southampton. This manufacturer built pioneering seaplanes designed to win the Schneider Trophy for the fastest aircraft in the world.

Mitchell's designs evolved from early, relatively clumsy models into sleek monoplanes and they won the trophy three times between 1927 and 1931. The 1931 winner was the S.6B, a Rolls-Royce-powered seaplane, whose elegant and slender form clearly anticipates the Spitfire. It won the trophy over a triangular course setting off from Portsmouth, achieving an average speed of 340.08 mph. A few weeks later, the plane became the first to break the 400-mph barrier.

'RJ', as the pipe-smoking Mitchell was known at Supermarine, had combined what John Vadar, the author of *Spitfire*, called 'sound knowledge with rare inspiration' to win the trophy. The Staffordshire-born designer, who left school at sixteen and whose first job was as an apprentice in a steam train engineering works, had become the leading aeronautical engineer of his generation. He was an early user of wind tunnel testing and watched the work of his mainly American and Italian rivals carefully to make use of their innovations, which he then adopted and improved.

In 1928 the Supermarine company had been taken over by Vickers Aviation and by 1930 the Air Ministry had issued a specification setting out the performance criteria for an all-metal, four-gun fighter with a short take-off run and a top speed of 250 mph. Mitchell was perfectly placed to take up the challenge, but his first attempt at a rudimentary fighter was a big disappointment.

The Supermarine Type 224, named the 'Spitfire' by the chairman of Vickers, Sir Robert McLean, was completed in 1934. It featured a previously untested steam-cooled Rolls-Royce Goshawk engine, chunky wings and a fixed undercarriage. However, it was slow compared with Mitchell's Schneider Trophy machines, reaching only 230 mph, and it lacked the agility he had hoped for.

Already suffering from the colon cancer that would kill him before he would ever see the Spitfire in combat, Mitchell went back to the drawing board, determined to produce a plane that far exceeded the ministry's ambitions. It would eventually emerge with the revolutionary Merlin engine from Rolls-Royce, which was to become the most famous airborne power unit of the Second World War.

The new fighter was developed without government money and retained the name Spitfire. It was the ailing Mitchell's personal response to what he could see from his visits to Germany was the growing menace of Nazi power.

Mitchell's goal was a fighter that would be characterised by its excellent aerodynamic and handling qualities, its strength and its speed, and he accurately anticipated its shape and performance well before the prototype came into being in 1935. This machine – with the serial number K5054 – featured the distinctive all-metal elliptical wings that Britons came to know and love, the narrow retractable undercarriage and an elegant and slender fuselage that owed its origins to the S.6B.

It was flown for the first time by the Vickers chief test pilot, J. 'Mutt' Summers, from Eastleigh airfield in Hampshire on a chilly morning on 5 March 1936. It was the first of 500 hours of testing as Mitchell worked to refine the plane and to make it faster; the team at Vickers worked their way through successive propeller designs and introduced flush-headed rivets into the fuselage to minimise drag. The Spitfire exceeded Mitchell's target of 350 mph by at least 12 mph.

There were concerns in the Air Ministry that Mitchell had produced what amounted to a rarefied Schneider Trophy aircraft that would be beyond the compass of ordinary RAF pilots. However, further trials convinced senior officers that the 'Spitfire 300', as it was then known, could be flown 'without risk by the average fully trained service fighter pilot'.

Mitchell died in 1937, aged forty-two, while still working to refine the aircraft and developing a new project – a four-engine bomber that never saw the light of day, after his drawings were destroyed in a bombing raid.

He had been awarded the CBE in 1932 for his work in designing ever-faster planes, but he has received no official honour for the critical part his Spitfire played in the defence of Britain in 1940 or its role throughout the Second World War. This is in marked contrast to Sydney Camm, the designer of the Hurricane, who was knighted in 1953.

Mitchell's career was dramatised in the 1942 film *The First of the Few*, while the story of his life was told by his son Gordon Mitchell in the book *R.J. Mitchell: Schooldays to Spitfire*. There is a statue of Mitchell standing at his drawing board at the Science Museum in London, commissioned by the American billionaire Sidney Frank. Yet efforts by his son – who died in 2009 – to have Mitchell honoured posthumously have been to no avail.

The first production order for the Spitfire was issued by the Air Ministry in June 1936 for 310 Mk Is that would fly in the Battle of Britain. They were armed with eight machine guns and powered by the Merlin II engine. Initial production of the ambitious and complex machine was relatively slow, so that by the end of 1938 only forty-nine aircraft had been delivered to the RAF; 19 Squadron was the first to fly them.

The Spitfire went on to become the most produced fighter in British history, with a total of 22,789 planes built as it evolved through nineteen 'Marks' and fifty-two variants. It played a key role in the Battle of Britain. On paper there was little to choose between the Spitfire and the Bf 109, so the advantage often went to the pilot with more experience or the one who was able to surprise his opponent.

While the fighter pilots fought it out in the skies over the English Channel, German bombers tried to destroy the Spitfire production line in Southampton. A number of successful bombing raids killed scores of experienced workers. However, the manufacturing process had already been outsourced to smaller units in the greater Southampton area and beyond, so the supply of planes continued.

After the Battle of Britain, the Spitfire superseded the Hurricane as the RAF's principal front-line fighter and it was deployed in all the main theatres of the Second World War in a variety of roles, including as an interceptor, as a fighter-bomber, for reconnaissance and as a training aircraft. The Supermarine Seafire was operated from aircraft carriers and made its debut in November 1942 during Operation Torch, the Allied landings in North Africa, and continued to be deployed throughout the war.

There have been numerous tributes to the Spitfire over the years, but one that stands out came in October 2016 from Mary Ellis. She flew seventy-six different types of aircraft and completed more than 1,000 flights delivering planes for the RAF during the Second World War.

Ogilvie on standby at Middle Wallop in 1940, and the inspirational Spitfire Mk I

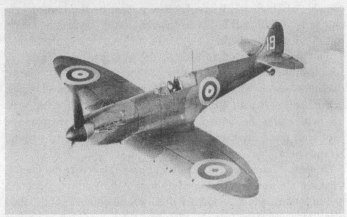

London burning after the raids on September 7, 1940

The former Air Transport Auxiliary pilot, who lived to the age of 101, flew 400 Spitfires and after being taken up in a two-seater version at the age of ninety-eight, she said: 'I love the Spitfire. It's everybody's favourite. I think it's a symbol of freedom.'

For Skeets Ogilvie, the Second World War provided a hell of a career. He distinguished himself as a Spitfire pilot in the Battle of Britain with six confirmed kills, another two probables and several more German aircraft damaged. He is celebrated as one of the RAF pilots involved in the shooting down of a Dornier 215 over central London a week after the events of 7 September.

On this occasion, Ogilvie attacked the plane – which had dropped two bombs on the forecourt of Buckingham Palace – three times from the side and then the rear, silencing the rear gunner and setting the cockpit on fire. The bomber then broke up and plummeted to the ground, landing on a jeweller's shop next to Victoria station.

The pilot of the German plane and two crew were killed, while two survivors parachuted on to the Kennington Oval cricket ground. The wreckage demolished the jeweller's shop and damaged the restaurant at Victoria station where thirty women were sheltering in the basement. Fortunately, no-one was injured.

Ogilvie's actions that day, in an incident that he always acknowledged involved other pilots, were witnessed by Queen Wilhelmina of the Netherlands who, together with other members of the Dutch royal family, stayed at Buckingham Palace for the duration of the war. She watched the drama unfolding in the skies above central London from the palace balcony.

In a note forwarded to 609 Squadron from her aide-de-camp she wrote: 'Her Majesty would be very pleased if Her congratulations should be conveyed to the Squadron concerned in the battle and to the pilot who shot down the German aircraft.'

The following July, and now at the controls of a Spitfire Mk V equipped with cannons, Ogilvie's luck ran out. Without any warning from his wingman, possibly because his radio was faulty, he was 'jumped' by a Bf 109 and shot down over France while escorting twelve Blenheim bombers attacking Lille.

'There was one hell of a "pow" and I was smacked into the dashboard, my port aileron floated away and a great rib appeared up my wing. I just could not believe it. I should have been covered by my section or warned. I can only imagine my radio chose this time to pack up,' he recalled.

Ogilvie tried to fly back towards the Channel as his instrument panel disintegrated. 'There was blood all over and I felt sick, so I blew my hood off and turned the oxygen on full to keep awake,' he said. In fact, he had suffered severe wounds to his back and left arm inflicted by two machine gun bullets and a cannon shell, and he managed to bail out shortly before his Spitfire caught fire.

After blacking out, Ogilvie came to in a field surrounded by French civilians, who did their best to patch him up before he was detained by a German soldier. He was taken by ambulance to a hospital in Lille. As one of his German captors put it: 'For you, the war is over!'

After a long convalescence, during which he received excellent treatment from Belgian and German doctors, Ogilvie was eventually transferred to the Stalag Luft III prisoner-of-war camp in Silesia. There he became the second-last man out of the tunnel from Hut 104 during the Great Escape on the night of 24 March 1944.

Ogilvie's luck may have deserted him over Lille, but it returned at this perilous moment: he was one of the twenty-three PoWs who were spared execution after all but three of the escapers were recaptured by the Germans.

He never knew for certain why he had not been shot, except that during his interrogation he made a point of underlining that he was a regular officer and he had not been involved in the digging of the tunnels, which was true. However, as one of the officers in charge of Red Cross parcels at the camp, he was always on the lookout for anything that could be of use in what became the most audacious escape attempt of the war.

Ogilvie had been spared death at the hands of the Gestapo, but his ordeal was far from over. Along with thousands of other prisoners, he endured what became known as the Long March in the first weeks of 1945, when thousands of ill-equipped prisoners were moved from eastern Germany and German-occupied Poland farther west to avoid being overrun by advancing Soviet troops. Many died along the way, mainly from the effects of cold, hunger and disease, or tragically, killed in 'friendly fire' incidents involving Allied aircraft.

Ogilvie survived this final gruelling test of his war and was eventually liberated at a camp near the Baltic coast in May 1945. On his return to Britain, he was hospitalised for two weeks while he was treated for a serious infection in his legs, contracted during life in camp and on the Long March.

After the war Ogilvie married Irene Lockwood, the daughter of British emigrants to Canada, who had returned to Britain in the 1930s. The couple first met in 1941, but they did not see each other for four more years while Ogilvie was a prisoner of war. During that time Irene worked for the postal and censorship branch of the Ministry of Information in London and then for the Royal Canadian Air Force (RCAF) as a staff photographer based in Britain. Immediately after the war, she toured the Continent with the RCAF's 'Carnival' roadshow, which entertained the troops.

While Irene became the love of his life, Ogilvie had at least one other serious girlfriend during the war who helped to keep his spirits up during his long captivity. His correspondence with Lilian Simpson, whom he met when his squadron moved to Biggin Hill aerodrome, south of London, in early 1941, is now on display at the new Biggin Hill Memorial Museum.

In one missive, dated 17 December 1942, a typically cheerful Ogilvie talks about the cold winter ahead in captivity:

Dear Lilian,
I have received your Christmas greetings and thank you for the kind thoughts. I trust you have by now received mine to you. We are preparing for a good Christmas and I'm sure we shall do very well. We are settling down now for a chilly winter and I hope to play a good bit of ice hockey on our rink. The arm is in good shape and should take it . . . . all the best and big love as ever.
    Keith

That relationship did not survive the vicissitudes of the end of the war as Ogilvie pursued Irene, travelling up to the Lake District to surprise her on holiday as soon as he was fit enough to do so. Happily married in Ottawa, Ogilvie and Irene – who died in 2014 – went on to have two children. Their son Keith became a pilot, gaining his private licence.

A great moment for father and son came when Keith took his father – who had long since retired from flying – up in his De Havilland Chipmunk, which had previously belonged to the Canadian Air Force (RCAF). Keith worked as an aerospace engineer in the RCAF and then with the Canadian space programme. Ogilvie's daughter, Jean, was a leadership coach.

In the years after the war, Skeets Ogilvie continued flying with the RCAF in a variety of transport and support roles, including flying the first jet supplied to the air force – the Canadian-built T-33 – which he described as humming 'like a vacuum cleaner'. He also flew the Vampire and F-86 Sabre.

After being appointed a staff officer at Air Materiel Command at Rockcliffe Air Base on the edge of Ottawa, his final role was as operations officer for an Air Transport base north of Toronto. Ogilvie retired from the RCAF in 1962 with nearly 5,000 hours in his logbook, including 300 in Spitfires. He subsequently worked for the Canadian government running a clerical office.

Ogilvie died in 1998, aged eighty-three. The quarterly newsletter from 609 Squadron paid this tribute to him. 'One of "The Few", we doubt his like will be seen again,' it said. 'They were an elite, men of high spirit, their comradeship forged by shared hazards and the intoxication of manning intricate, almost invincible, machines.'

There is a fitting tribute to him at the RAF Museum at Hendon in north London, which has on permanent display the Spitfire Mk 1 – Serial No. X4590 – that Ogilvie flew from Middle Wallop with 609 Squadron in November 1940.

In its detailed history of the plane, the museum includes this entry for 28 November 1940:

Yellow section scramble; pilot P/O Hill, taking off at 10.35 and landing at 11.00. Also later that day, Pilot Officer Ogilvie, flying X4590 as Yellow 3, was scrambled at 13.35 and returned at 14.55, only to be scrambled again at 15.50 in X4590 and vectored towards the Solent to intercept a formation of Me 109s of JG2 led by Major Helmut Wick. The Germans had the height advantage and bounced the Spitfires; Ogilvie escaped in a damaged X4590, as recorded in his diary; 'I was Yellow 3 and was weaving merrily behind, keeping an eagle eye above, when I caught a glimpse of three yellow noses in my mirror. They were obviously crack pilots by their tight formation and strategy. I gave the warning and dove as the centre Johnny opened fire on me, and was speeded on my way by a cannon shell up the fuselage and a second through my prop. Returned to base at 16.55.'

Anthony 'Steady' Tuke flew more than 100 combat missions, including attacks on German shipping earmarked for the invasion of Britain, and was twice awarded the DSC for his courage in action

13

Sub-Lieutenant Anthony 'Steady' Tuke
Fairey Albacore Torpedo Bomber

11 September 1940

*The first I knew about it was tracer bullets
passing either side of my head.*

F OUR YEARS AFTER winning the Distinguished Service Cross at
the height of the Battle of Britain, Anthony Tuke was struggling
to deal with the mental consequences of aerial combat. He had
been on the front line since he was nineteen.

A candid and courageous man, Tuke admitted years later: 'I
wanted the war to end as soon as possible, I'd had enough . . . I
must admit that during the last part of the war I had what we called
"twitch". I didn't think I could go on.'

Twitch was RAF slang for body tremors that afflicted aircrew
suffering from operational stress. The symptoms were familiar to
men serving with both the RAF and the Luftwaffe – and sometimes
the remedies used were similar, too.

In the summer of 1940, the modern phrase 'flying high' could
have applied, in some cases, literally and figuratively. Some pilots
came to rely on alcohol and drugs, the former to relieve tension
and to help deal with fear, the latter to stave off tiredness. For the
RAF in south-east England, it was predominantly beer and Pimm's;
for the Luftwaffe crews in northern France and the Low Countries,
it was wine and schnapps.

A bluff heartiness often masked the anxieties of pilots, who faced
the real prospect of being burnt alive or seriously disfigured if they
survived. RAF crews referred to fallen comrades as having 'Gone

for a Burton', which was a morbid conflation of going out for a beer – a Burton Ale – and going out for ever.

According to Sinclair McKay, the author of *The Secret Life of Fighter Command*: 'The drinking stories – the rural taverns, the cheerful after-hours lock-ins, the beer and whisky, the enormous quantities consumed – make you wonder how these men could possibly function before dawn the next day. Many of them must surely have been drunk come first light. Perhaps for some that was the best way to approach the next day's flying.'

Doctors on both sides prescribed amphetamines. Benzedrine was dispensed to RAF pilots and members of the Women's Auxiliary Air Force (WAAF) working in the operations rooms to help them stave off fatigue. Across the Channel, the Germans used a stronger drug, Pervitin, which was essentially crystal meth, and became known as 'pilot's chocolate'.

The drug had a profound effect on Luftwaffe pilots, giving them seemingly 'superhuman resistance' to tiredness, but it was not long before troubling elements of drug use became apparent: an inability to sleep, psychotic phases and even suicides. And then there were the troubling side effects of addiction, ranging from hallucinations to depression, which could last for years if the airman survived.

Like many pilots, Tuke suffered from the stresses of flying on the aerial front line, but the young British pilot faced his fears and would live to nearly ninety. In the course of flying 110 combat sorties, he was twice awarded the DSC, which recognises acts of exemplary gallantry against the enemy at sea. He was also given a nickname that became renowned throughout the Fleet Air Arm. He was 'Steady' – Anthony 'Steady' Tuke.

The name first arose during training, when instructors constantly referred to his progress on Tiger Moths as 'steady'. A fellow pilot acclaimed him as such – 'Oh Steady!' – after he suddenly stopped drinking at a party because his final flying test was the next day. It remained with him all his life, and in old age he still laughed about the epithet.

Tuke had joined 826 Naval Air Squadron, which was equipped with Fairey Albacore torpedo bombers, at Ford aerodrome in Sussex in April 1940. Shortly afterwards, the teenage pilot was in action, flying the slow, outdated biplane against the Luftwaffe's modern fighters.

Known by its crews as the 'Applecore', the aircraft was a single-engine bomber designed to fly from aircraft carriers; it was created in response to a government specification for a 'three-seat torpedo/spotter/reconnaissance aircraft' to replace the better known Fairey Swordfish, which had been introduced in 1936, but looked like one of the flying machines left over from the First World War.

Designed by Marcelle Lobelle, a Belgian aeronautical engineer who worked for the Fairey aviation company, the Albacore first flew in the winter of 1938–39. Unlike the Swordfish, it had an enclosed cockpit, and a modern life-raft ejection system that was triggered if the aircraft ditched in the sea.

In most other respects, the Albacore offered little if any improvement on the Swordfish, which was more manoeuvrable, with lighter controls. Both aircraft, however, raised questions about the standard of procurement at a time when other countries were producing faster, more advanced aircraft for combat at sea.

The Albacore had a cruising speed of 140 mph and a top speed of 160 mph. This gave it one unexpected advantage in combat; modern fighters such as the Messerschmitt Bf 109 found it difficult to attack the British bomber because it was so slow, and they would sometimes overshoot the target. It was armed with three machine guns, one on the starboard wing and two at the back of an elongated cockpit, and it could carry one torpedo or four 500lb bombs or depth charges. The aircraft could also be used as a dive bomber.

In May 1940, Tuke's squadron was posted to Detling in Kent, where they flew in support of Operation Dynamo, the evacuation of the British Expeditionary Force from Dunkirk. They were briefly based in Jersey, where the crews practised night flying – 'The locals were very cross,' he said, 'we kept them awake!' – shortly before the German occupation of the island.

Later the Albacores moved to Bircham Newton in Norfolk, attacking the advancing German forces in north-west Europe, laying mines and protecting British convoys. On the last day of May, they bombed road and rail targets at Westende and attacked E-boats off the Belgian coast at Zeebrugge.

After laying mines in Dutch canals on the night of 26 June, Tuke's Albacore suffered engine failure, but he guided it back to Britain in a glide over the shoreline before crash-landing in the dunes at Waxham Sands on the Norfolk coast. His aircraft was badly damaged, but he and his crew emerged unharmed. The raid was however a taste of difficult encounters ahead.

On 11 September 1940, Tuke and his crew manned one of six Albacores from 826 squadron given the task of attacking a convoy of invasion barges off Calais. Anyone listening to Churchill's radio broadcast to the nation on the same day could be under no illusions about the importance of Tuke's task.

Churchill told his audience that 'the effort of the Germans to secure mastery of the air over England is of course the crux of the whole war' and that to try to invade without having secured such mastery would be hazardous.

The British prime minister acknowledged, however, that Hitler's 'preparations for invasion on a great scale are steadily moving forward'. Hundreds of self-propelled barges were being moved down the coast of Europe from German and Dutch harbours to the ports of northern France. Other shipping was building up, too. Large numbers of German troops awaited Hitler's order.

'No one should blind himself to the fact that a heavy full-scale invasion of this island is being prepared with all the usual German thoroughness and method, and that it may be launched now,' Churchill said.

'Therefore, we must regard the next week or so as a very important period in our history. It ranks with the days when the Spanish Armada was approaching the Channel, and Drake was finishing his game of bowls; or when Nelson stood between us and Napoleon's Grand Army at Boulogne.'

In an all-embracing pronouncement, Churchill added: 'Every man and every woman will therefore prepare himself to do his duty, whatever it may be, with special pride and care.'

On that fine, sunny afternoon, Anthony Tuke flew in a formation of six Albacores towards the French port, escorted by six twin-engine Blenheim Mk IV fighters from 235 Squadron, which had taken off from Detling at 3.55 p.m.

While approaching France at about 10,000ft, Tuke could see a number of Bf 109s taking off from the small grass airfield at Calais. 'Three minutes later they were behind us,' he recalled.

Flying an Albacore with the serial number M-Monkey, Tuke

tried to outmanoeuvre the German fighters, jinking his aircraft and then slowing down, while the Blenheims desperately tried to defend the Fleet Air Arm bombers. According to 235 Squadron's combat reports, a Blenheim was 'shot down in flames' by a Bf 109, but one of the plane's gunners, Sergeant Watts, 'was seen to continue firing until the aircraft fell into the sea'.

About two dozen aircraft were involved in the clash over Calais. The Albacores were first attacked by enemy flak as they descended to 8,000ft over the French port. Then they were confronted by the fighters. Tuke's gunner, Naval Airman Robert Matthews, started firing his machine guns.

In a gravelly, sometimes hesitant voice recorded by the Imperial War Museum in 2006, Tuke recalled his first encounter with the Luftwaffe. 'The first I knew about it,' he said, 'was tracer bullets passing through [the cockpit] either side of my head . . . they damaged the engine, the air gunner was injured in the shoulder, and the observer, Edgar Brown, got it in the head.'

According to one report, the main spar of Tuke's aircraft was shot away. The upper aileron jammed. The petrol tank was holed. Both tyres were punctured.

Tuke knew that he had to get away if he was to survive. 'There was one cloud in the sky I reckon, so I headed for that, I thought that would be somewhere to hide . . . I dropped all my bombs over the sea and then headed as fast as I could back to the coast.'

After guiding his battered Albacore back to Norfolk, Tuke landed the aircraft in spite of all the damage it had sustained. 'I was better off than one chap who had lost one wheel,' he said. 'There was quite a reception party.' An ambulance was waiting to deal with his wounded crew. One of the senior pilots complained that Tuke had taken his cloud. 'I didn't argue with them,' he said.

When asked years later about his own state after the raid, he said: 'I wasn't hurt at all,' and laughed. 'I would have been if I'd turned my head an inch either way.'

After the raid, Tuke's courage was recognised. 'That's when I got my first DSC,' he said. The award was announced in the *London Gazette* on 13 November 1940. He also kept one of the spent shells from the aircraft's machine guns and gave it to his sister as a memento.

The raid was not a success. The Albacores never found the convoy of invasion barges. One of the squadron's aircraft was shot down and three more were badly damaged. Two of the Blenheims escorting the bomber force were also destroyed. The Luftwaffe lost one of its fighters in the engagement and Goering is reported to have complained about its failure to wipe out a force of 'old prewar biplanes'.

Among the casualties that day was Frederick Flood, an Australian who had joined 235 squadron as a flight commander in June and had been in action throughout the Battle of Britain. His body was never found and he was officially 'presumed' dead on 2 July 1941, after his family in Queensland had been waiting for news of him for nearly a year. His personal effects were lost in transit aboard the SS *Ceramic* while being returned to Australia. The ship was torpedoed by a German U-boat on 6 December 1942.

Many other people lost their lives on 11 September 1940. German bombers flying in two waves – about 300 escorted by fighters – were detected by British radar stations during the early afternoon. The Luftwaffe was using massed formations that crossed the Kent coast and headed for London along the River Thames.

Air Vice-Marshal Keith Park, head of 11 Group, mobilised his fighter squadrons in pairs and brought in reinforcements. He ordered the faster Spitfires to attack the German fighters and the Hurricanes to concentrate on the bombers. For those on the ground, vapour trails, like brushstrokes on a great canvas, provided a picture of the fighting at high altitude.

To the west, Portsmouth and Southampton also came under attack. Liverpool and Bristol were hit. Later that night, the bombers returned to London as the Blitz gathered force. Buckingham Palace was damaged, much to the apparent relief of Queen Elizabeth, who said: 'I feel now that I can look the people of the East End straight in the eye.'

According to the Battle of Britain Historical Society, the RAF sustained greater losses than the Luftwaffe for the first time. Fighter Command flew 678 sorties and lost twenty-nine aircraft, with seventeen pilots killed and six wounded. The Luftwaffe lost twenty-five aircraft, but many suffered damage and claims made by the RAF at the time were much higher. On the ground, a total of 1,211 civilians – 976 in London – were killed in the week ending 11 September.

Tuke was involved in no further operations for more than two weeks, because the squadron was short of aircraft after being so badly shot up – but his war had only just begun.

In December, 826 Squadron joined the aircraft carrier HMS *Formidable* and sailed round the Cape of Good Hope to the Suez Canal. On the way, Tuke was involved in attacks on Italian forces at Mogadishu and Massawa in east Africa.

He was in action again in March 1941 at the Battle of Cape Matapan, when British and Australian forces engaged the Italian fleet off the south-west coast of Greece. The Albacores made repeated attacks and torpedoed the 40,000-ton *Vittorio Veneto*, hitting her rudder.

'At one point we thought we had possibly sunk the Italian battleship,' Tuke said, 'but we obviously hadn't, because she turned up again later.' The Italians nevertheless lost three heavy cruisers and two destroyers in the engagement.

Two months later, the *Formidable* was badly damaged by Stukas during the evacuation from Crete. Tuke survived. He then operated from El Adem, south of Tobruk, in Libya, escorting convoys through the Mediterranean. These missions included Operation Tiger, which brought tanks, Hurricanes packed in crates, and other vital supplies to Alexandria for the Eighth Army. Tuke was later deployed to the Western Desert, often operating as a dive bomber as Allied forces held back Rommel in the summer of 1942.

After returning to England, Tuke was appointed 'senior pilot' with 819 Squadron, which was equipped with the old 'Stringbag', as the Swordfish was known by its crews. He flew for three months with Coastal Command, once again attacking German shipping in European ports, and laying mines, but this time at night. In February 1943, the squadron joined the escort carrier HMS *Archer* and provided cover against U-boats for two Atlantic convoys.

For the young Tuke, still only twenty-two, there would be no let-up. A veteran of considerable experience, he was promoted to acting lieutenant-commander, given command of 851 Squadron and deployed to the US naval air station at Squantum in Massachusetts to convert to a new, modern aircraft: the American-made Grumman Avenger torpedo bomber.

Sent to the Indian Ocean on the escort carrier, HMS *Shah*, Tuke

Tuke, bottom right, in 1938; and with Frances on their wedding day.
Albacores on HMS Formidable

spotted *U-198* on 10 August 1944 and attacked the German submarine, which had sailed out of La Pallice in France and had recently sunk four merchant ships. Tuke failed to sink the U-boat and then took part in a two-day search. She was attacked again north of the Seychelles by the Indian sloop HMIS *Godavari* and the frigate HMS *Findhorn* with depth charges. There were no survivors among the German crew.

For his part in the action, Tuke was awarded a bar to his DSC for what *The Daily Telegraph* described as his 'courage, leadership and determination', his last significant act in combat.

He did find one more target, however. Having been rested and put in command of flying at the deck training school at HMS *Peewit*, north of Edinburgh, his eyes settled on the captain's secretary, third officer Frances Harvey WRNS. His affections were returned; she accepted his hand in marriage.

Fittingly, Tuke's life had started with strong maritime connections. He had been born Anthony Montague Tuke on 28 December 1920, at St Albans, Hertfordshire, where his mother, Gladys, was staying with friends. His father was Captain Rowland Tuke, a senior officer in the Merchant Navy. Captain Tuke went to sea on the day his son was born and did not see him for three weeks. The family home was at Boxford in Suffolk.

Anthony was sent to board at Woodbridge School, and there he flourished. He was captain of rugby, cricket, tennis and fives, became company sergeant-major in the Officer Training Corps, and head boy, but he was not always so self-assured in the classroom. Later in life he returned there as a governor.

He had his first taste of flying with a freelance pilot, who went around the country offering flights for five shillings. 'That convinced me that flying was what I wanted,' Tuke said.

He joined the Royal Navy in 1938 and learnt to fly a Tiger Moth at the naval air school at Gravesend. 'The idea of being in the navy and flying was ideal,' he said. 'The Tiger Moth was great fun, you could do anything in it; it was a wonderful aircraft.'

And then the country went to war. 'I was excited,' Tuke said. He went home on leave and recalled talking in a shop, buying cigarettes. 'I said, "I expect it'll be over by next Christmas!"'

The war took its toll, though.

According to Tuke's son Adam: 'The subject of mental stress or fatigue is very pertinent in the current climate, although previous generations tended to ignore it wherever possible. Dad clearly did suffer from the twitch, as he readily admitted in later life, but I'm sure at the time he and others tried to gloss over such symptoms. I do know that in September 1944 he returned from a patrol to HMS *Shah* and the ship's medical officer met him and grounded him straight away, saying his war was over.'

After the war, Tuke commanded 783 Squadron at the Naval Air Signal School at Arbroath until November 1947, when he was discharged without a pension, which rankled for the rest of his life.

As Adam said: 'He was obviously extremely proud of his naval service and loyal to the Fleet Air Arm, but he was always bitter about his treatment at the end. Although he had been in the navy for the required length of time to qualify for a pension, he was told that his service prior to being commissioned did not count. He was chucked out with a £200 gratuity [worth about £8,200 today] and no other training or qualification to fall back on and with a wife and young son to provide for.'

He wanted to buy a farm, but never had enough money. Instead, he became group secretary for the West Essex branch of the National Farmers' Union and a tax commissioner. He and Frances had two sons, Tim, who joined the navy and later worked as an engineer, and Adam, who became a civil engineering contractor.

Tuke supported squadron reunions and Fleet Air Arm dinners almost until his death at the age of eighty-nine in 2010. He never complained about the war and remained very much in character – 'steady' to the end.

A memorial to the Polish fighter pilot Boleslaw Wlasnowolski in the Sussex field where his Hurricane crashed. He was killed far from home, after being shot down while he should have been on leave

14

Pilot Officer Boleslaw Wlasnowolski
Hawker Hurricane Single-Engine Fighter

15 September 1940

The aircraft had one serious drawback:
the proximity of the fuel tanks to the cockpit.

IN THE ROLLING chalk hills of the South Downs, a few miles north of the former RAF aerodrome at Tangmere near Chichester, a windswept cornfield bears testimony to the courage of a young Polish fighter pilot flying far from home. A simple plaque bears the name of Pilot Officer Boleslaw Wlasnowolski.

Walk across the Downs today and you can sometimes still hear the deep, rich rhythms of a Rolls-Royce Merlin engine as a Spitfire from Goodwood passes overhead. Nearly eighty years after the battle, it remains a distinctly spiritual experience.

In the summer of 1940, Pilot Officer Wlasnowolski, nicknamed 'Vodka' by his fellow RAF airmen, was twenty-three years old. The year before, he had been one of the first pilots to confront the Nazis when the Germans invaded his homeland. He then escaped after his country was overrun and a year later, flying with the RAF, he helped to inflict a formidable toll on the Luftwaffe at the height of the Battle of Britain.

The middle of September 1940 marked the most intense phase of the battle. It was at this stage that the Luftwaffe launched its heaviest attacks on London, culminating on 15 September in a raid that Hitler hoped would turn the course of the war in Germany's favour, and create the conditions for the invasion of Britain.

The ferocious aerial combat that day, which involved 1,700 aircraft, has since been commemorated in Britain and elsewhere among her allies as 'Battle of Britain Day'. Fighter Command was severely stretched as hundreds of German bombers made the best of fine daylight flying conditions over southern England to press home their attack. Twenty-nine Allied fighters were lost and twenty-one damaged in the combat, while the Germans lost at least fifty-seven aircraft, with a further twenty severely damaged. At the time the RAF claimed that more than 170 enemy aircraft had been destroyed.

On that day Wlasnowolski was at the controls of the RAF's most prolific fighter, the Hawker Hurricane. In the popular imagination the Hurricane has always been eclipsed by the Spitfire, its more agile and glamorous successor, but the Hurricane inflicted 60 per cent of the losses sustained by the Luftwaffe during the Battle of Britain.

The Hurricane developed out of the Hawker Fury biplane, an RAF fighter from the early 1930s. Designed by Sydney Camm, the aircraft first flew on 6 November 1935, while Wlasnowolski was still at school. Camm was a British aeronautical engineer, who had started work during the First World War and created not only the Hurricane, but later the Tempest and Typhoon, which also left their mark on aviation history.

The Hurricane cost about £6,000 in 1939 (about £400,000 today) and it was a considerable step forward in both design and performance. It was a single-seater monoplane interceptor aircraft with retractable undercarriage, powered by a Merlin engine, which could reach speeds of 315 mph and climb from take-off to 15,000ft in less than six minutes. It was equipped with eight remotely operated, wing-mounted Browning machine guns, designed for conducting rapid engagements.

The early versions of the Hurricane were heavily influenced by methods of biplane construction, with a wood and canvas airframe and wings. However, by 1940 the wings were being built with metal skins that improved the aircraft's diving speed. It was agile enough to compete with some German fighters, but it was slower than its main adversary, the Messerschmitt Bf 109. The Hurricane's strength was that it could out-turn its German counterpart, as indeed it could a Spitfire, which was a critical advantage for pilots with hostile planes on their tails.

By the end of the Battle of France and the evacuation of British forces from Dunkirk, the Hurricane had already made a huge contribution to Britain's war effort. Squadrons equipped with the aircraft are believed to have shot down about 400 German planes during the Battle of France – and lost a similar number of their own, many of them on the ground. More than three-quarters of a century later, the figures are difficult to verify.

On the eve of the Battle of Britain in July 1940, just over half of Fighter Command's sixty-one squadrons were equipped with Hurricanes. These were often deployed against the Luftwaffe's bombers, while the Spitfires were left to take on the German fighters.

For its pilots, the aircraft had one serious drawback: the proximity of the fuel tanks to the cockpit meant that the young men who flew them could quickly become engulfed in flames when the aircraft, with its wood and canvas fuselage, was hit. Many were left with serious burns to their faces and upper bodies.

This was not, however, to be the fate of Wlasnowolski on 15 September. Billeted among unfamiliar comrades from 607 Squadron at his new base at Tangmere, he scrambled his Hurricane and joined the interception of German squadrons over the south coast, only a few minutes from his own airfield. In the subsequent engagement, the young Pole shot down a Dornier 17 bomber, his fourth confirmed kill of the war.

His official combat report, held in the National Archives, seems almost brutal in its description of the destruction of the Dornier and its crew, and reads like an old-fashioned telegram from the front line. Wlasnowolski wrote:

I was Red 3, flying in section 2. From this position, saw Do 17 at about 12,000ft flying alone to my right over coast near Poole. Pursued enemy aircraft who tried to escape by taking zig-zag course above cloud. Fired two bursts [from 200 yards] from behind and a little below. Saw engine catch fire and E/A [enemy aircraft] dived below thin cloud. I followed him down and saw E/A dive into sea in flames and sink. Enemy pilot sunk with plane. After this, having become detached from section rejoined base alone.

Wlasnowolski was typical of the Polish pilots who flew in the Battle of Britain, many of them with considerable training and operational experience. Fired by the desire to avenge the invasion of their homeland, these young men demonstrated exceptional bravery. Indeed, they were noted for flying so close to the enemy during engagements that they often seemed in danger of colliding with their adversaries, before raking them with machine gun bullets.

Of the Polish pilots who found a new base in Britain from which to fight, 139 flew with the RAF between 10 July and 31 October, when the battle is officially regarded by the British as having ended. And it was a Polish squadron, 303, that achieved the most kills, with 201 victories.

Boleslaw Andrzej Wlasnowolski – his surname means 'from his own field' or 'domain' – was born on 29 November 1916, in Krakow, the son of Wladyslaw, a railway clerk, and his wife, Maria. He had one elder brother, Julek, who became a surgeon, and an elder sister, Ania. A good-looking boy with chestnut hair, Wlasnowolski was popular within his wider family and is remembered as warm and friendly. He graduated from the Henryk Sienkiewicz secondary school in 1936 and, a year later, joined the air force cadet school at Deblin, having set his heart on flying from a young age.

In June 1939, barely three months before the outbreak of the Second World War, Wlasnowolski joined 122 Squadron of the Polish Air Force in Krakow. They were equipped with fourteen single-wing, all-metal fighters (PZL P11s) that had been the envy of the military aviation world in the early 1930s. But, by the time of the German invasion of Poland, they were outclassed by the new Luftwaffe aircraft.

The Polish Air Force managed to inflict considerable losses on the Germans, despite flying relatively slow planes. Wlasnowolski is credited with a shared kill with Wladyslaw Majchrzyk on 2 September, when they shot down a Stuka dive bomber, the great icon of the Blitzkreig. The German plane crashed two miles east of the little-known town of Oswiecim, now infamous around the world as Auschwitz. The Stuka's pilot, believed to be Heinz Werner, and his radio operator, Arthur Otto, were both killed.

With the defeat of Poland all but certain, Wlasnowolski had, by 17 September, escaped with his squadron to Romania. He then travelled to France and on to England, where he arrived in January 1940, and promptly enlisted in the Royal Air Force Volunteer Reserve as a 'Pilot Officer on Probation'. He was given the service number 76736. Majchrzyk also escaped to Britain and fought with the Allies throughout the war.

After intensive training – having mastered the Hurricane in 15 days rather than the allotted three months – Wlasnowolski joined 32 Squadron at Biggin Hill in August. Flying alongside him were two other Polish pilots, Jan Pfeiffer, who was known as 'Fife', and Karol Pniak, who was nicknamed 'Cognac'. As with 'Vodka' Wlasnowolski, the monikers appear to have had little to do with their drinking habits and were solely a means of simplifying their names. In other squadrons, Stanislaw Brzezina was known as 'Breezy' and Henryk Szczesny as 'Sneezy'.

No. 32 was one of the most successful Hurricane squadrons in the RAF and Pniak quickly made his mark, becoming an ace by adding three new kills to the two he had achieved in Poland. Wlasnowolski found it more difficult to adjust to life in the RAF – and to fighting in the Battle of Britain. His first flight from Biggin Hill ended with his Hurricane overshooting the runway on landing and careering into a garden just outside the perimeter. His first combat sortie ended in a similar manner in a field near Dover.

Then, on 15 August, he shot down his first enemy aircraft over Britain during a sortie that ended with another crash-landing, this time in a field in Essex, with the impact destroying the undercarriage.

'I spotted nine Me 109s above me in V formation,' he recalled afterwards. 'I climbed and attacked one from behind. We started to circle when the Messerschmitt dived. I sent him a good burst and it started to burn and was diving towards the sea. I turned back towards the other [enemy planes], but I was unable to catch up with any.'

Wlasnowolski had further success on 18 August, when he downed a Dornier bomber in the morning and in the afternoon jointly shot down a Bf 109 with Flight Lieutenant Peter Brothers over Canterbury.

A Hurricane being re-armed; and pilots scrambling; Wlasnowolski, crosslegged, far right, with pilots of 32 Squadron

The Polish pilot was reported to have used only four short bursts from his guns to disable the German plane.

Two days after 15 September, Wlasnowolski was transferred to 213 Squadron, which was based at Tangmere. Exactly a month later, he claimed what was to be his final victory in the Battle of Britain when he shot down another Bf 109, giving him five kills in all and making him a fighter ace.

On 1 November, the day after the Battle of Britain is now recognised to have ended, Wlasnowolski received his posting to an all-Polish fighter squadron. He was due to take some leave, having flown continuously throughout the battle since the middle of August. However, a new squadron leader arrived that day to take over 213 and instructed Wlasnowolski and another Polish pilot to remain 'on readiness' in case of a German attack, because of a shortage of pilots.

At about 3 p.m. that afternoon, the Luftwaffe appeared in the sky over Tangmere. Wlasnowolski and ten other pilots scrambled to meet them. In the ensuing melee, Wlasnowolski was shot down by Hermann Reiff-Erscheidt in his Bf 109. The young Pole's fighter came down in flames at about 4 p.m., crashing into a hedge on the edge of a field near the village of Stoughton, about seven miles north-west of Tangmere.

It is thought that Wlasnowolski was killed instantly on impact, or he may have been dead in his cockpit before the plane hit the ground. His body was recovered and is buried in Chichester cemetery. He was posthumously awarded the War Order of Virtuti Militari – Poland's highest military award for heroism in the face of the enemy.

His story may well have faded with the passage of time, had it not been for Ronald Langmead, who owned the beautiful chalk farmland on the South Downs where Wlasnowolski's aircraft crashed. In the late 1990s, Langmead recovered several fragments of the downed Hurricane, and resolved to honour the Polish pilot who had died on his land in 1940.

On the footpath next to the field where the plane came down, Langmead commissioned a simple memorial with a plaque on a granite plinth that faces across the field to the hedge where Wlasnowolski died. The legend reads:

★

In this field, on 1st November 1940

Pilot Officer Bolesław Własnowolski V.M., K.W.

Royal Air Force
213 SQUADRON R.A.F. TANGMERE
(formerly of the Polish Air Force)

Died aged 23 when his "Hurricane" V7221
crashed following aerial combat
with a German Me 109

HE DIED DEFENDING BRITAIN, POLAND
AND FREEDOM

Langmead not only commissioned the monument, but he installed two granite benches alongside it – with stone ordered from Cornwall – so that visitors have somewhere to sit as they contemplate the fate of this fine-featured Pole.

According to Langmead's widow, Joan, they placed a small advertisement in the local paper announcing that the plaque would be officially unveiled on 25 July 1997. They were astonished when more than 200 people – many of them Polish – turned up. Among those present were members of the Własnowolski family, who had flown from Poland, representatives of the Polish Air Force Association, Monsignor Tadeusz Kukla of the Polish Catholic Chaplaincy in London, who led a short service, and two children dressed in Polish national costume.

Another figure in attendance was an ageing air marshal, Sir Frederick Sowrey, who flew reconnaissance missions over occupied Europe after 1942. He spoke of the plight of Poland at the outset of the war, the stubborn fight put up by her air force and the odyssey by land and sea of men like Wlasnowolski, who were determined to reach Britain and fly again.

After the unveiling of the memorial, which had been covered in the Polish flag, and the laying of wreaths and flowers, those present made their way back to Church Farm in the village, where fragments of the Hurricane had been collected and presented on a large table in the centre of the lawn. 'We then proceeded downhill to the assembly areas where many tables, covered with white and red checked cloths, were laden with sandwiches, cakes and tea,' recalled Langmead.

The Hurricane flew throughout the Second World War and after the Battle of Britain it became Fighter Command's main single-engine night-fighter during the Blitz. The aircraft continued to evolve in design, performance and armament and was deployed variously as a bomber-interceptor, fighter-bomber and ground support aircraft in addition to its original role as a fighter aircraft. The naval version, the Sea Hurricane, operated from Royal Navy carriers from mid-1941.

Hurricanes featured in the European theatre, but also in North Africa against the Italian air force, in the defence of Malta, in the Far East and the Soviet Union. By the end of production in July 1944, a total of 14,487 Hurricanes had been built in Britain and Canada, the majority (9,986) by Hawker at Brooklands in Surrey, with 2,750 built by the Gloster Aircraft Company, a Hawker subsidiary. A further 1,451 were built by the Canadian Car & Foundry at Fort William in Ontario.

The Canadian Hurricanes were produced under the direction of Elsie MacGill, the chief engineer at Canadian Car & Foundry and among the first women in the world to earn an aeronautical engineering degree. She introduced refinements to the aircraft, including skis and de-icing gear for winter operations, and was dubbed the 'Queen of the Hurricanes'.

It is not known what Pilot Officer Wlasnowolski thought of Camm's aircraft – or even how he lived and perhaps loved during the months he spent in Britain. There are no letters or personal papers available for research, but perhaps one day some may come to light, left in a long-forgotten drawer. The few photographs of him show an intense young man, a patriot and Polish warrior, whose deeds left their mark in the cornfields of the English Downs – and far beyond.

Fritz Ruhlandt showed great skill in landing his Junkers 88 on Graveney Marshes. Accounts of his crew's clashes with the London Irish Rifles read like an episode of the TV show Dad's Army

15

Sergeant Fritz Ruhlandt
Junkers 88 A1 Fast Medium Bomber

27 September 1940

We gave the Germans pints of beer
in exchange for a few souvenirs.

FRITZ RUHLANDT KNEW that his brand-new Junkers 88, nick-named the Owl, was in trouble. A veteran of the campaigns in Poland and France, the German pilot and his crew of three had dropped their 4,000lb cargo of bombs over London and were heading east over the Thames estuary and northern Kent on their way back to France.

One of their engines had been hit by anti-aircraft fire from a gun emplacement at Upnor Castle beside the Medway, and they were being harried by Spitfires just south of the Isle of Sheppey.

According to Erwin Richter, a radio operator and air gunner on board the stricken aircraft: 'We were separated from our unit formation and were immediately attacked by three fighters.'

Richter, who had already won an Iron Cross and had recently married, tried to keep the fighters at bay, but the Ju 88 was seriously outgunned. At least one burst of fire grazed the aircraft's canopy.

'Ruhlandt dived at once, and as he neared the ground, he found that the second engine had failed,' recalled Richter. 'There was no longer any opportunity to get out [with a parachute], as we were too near the ground. So, we had to make an emergency landing.'

According to one report, Eddy Goodwin, a labourer, was working at Monks Hill Farm when he heard the sound of gunfire and saw the Ju 88 losing height over the village of Graveney. Another witness reported that as the aircraft passed over Odding Path, the crew were seen to jettison the damaged cockpit canopy, which narrowly missed hitting another farm worker called Jack Gurr.

The bomber then flew low over Graveney Hill before touching down and coming to rest by the sea wall. It was a few hundred yards west-south-west of the Sportsman Inn at Seasalter, a hamlet on the north coast of Kent near Faversham.

Ruhlandt had managed to land his crippled bomber with 'commendable skill'. One witness said: 'The Ju 88 bellied in, bouncing and slithering some 300 yards on the soft ground of the marsh, jumping a ditch and shearing off both propellers before slewing to a stop some quarter mile from the Sportsman.'

The scene was now set for a clash of arms that is still celebrated in these parts of Kent as 'The Battle of Graveney Marshes', an encounter between Ruhlandt and his crew – Erwin Richter; the observer Gotthard Richter; and Jakob Reiner, an air gunner who was operating the rear-facing machine guns – and a platoon from A Company, the 1st Battalion London Irish Rifles.

The Rifles, who were part of the country's preparations to meet a German invasion through the south-east corner of England, had the good fortune to be billeted in the Sportsman, which specialised in local seafood, particularly oysters from beds about a mile offshore.

To some commentators, the 'battle' was no more than an unremarkable skirmish; after all, nine other Ju 88s had been brought down over Gravesend the previous week.

To others – possibly fortified by the Guinness that was readily available at the Sportsman, a hostelry dating back to 1642 that is still serving beer today – it became a legend. It was, they say, the first battle between warring nations to be fought on British soil since – and this depends on your choice of history book – Bonnie Prince Charlie's defeat at Culloden in 1746 or the Battle of Fishguard in 1797, when a detachment of soldiers from revolutionary France was seen off in south-west Wales before they could fire a shot.

So frequent were the air battles in this part of the country in 1940 that the soldiers of the London Irish Rifles gave this one barely a passing thought. Instead, A Company was spending that afternoon preparing for its regular pay parade and weapons inspection.

War Substantive Lieutenant (temporary Captain) John Kelly Cantopher had arrived at the Sportsman to take the inspection, but then noticed that the German aircraft was coming down close by. He was also apparently aware that the aircraft, characterised by its extended wings, improved handling and upgraded navigational aids, was a new model and that the RAF wanted to capture one more or less intact, to study its secrets.

Ruhlandt's aircraft was a Ju 88 A1, one of the latest and finest bombers in the Luftwaffe's fleet. It had been completed at the end of July and had entered service only two weeks previously.

The military historian Andy Saunders records in his book *Arrival of Eagles: Luftwaffe Landings in Britain 1939–45* that on getting to the pub, Cantopher mentioned the downing of the German aircraft to a Sergeant Allworth.

'Yes, sir!' replied Allworth. 'I have sent some men.'

According to Saunders, Cantopher glanced at the weaponry laid out for inspection by the Rifles, and brusquely asked: 'They took arms, I hope?'

Allworth, snapping to attention, barked: 'No, sir. [It's] the arms inspection, sir!'

No sooner were the words out of the platoon sergeant's mouth than the sounds of short bursts of machine gun fire rang out across the fields. 'It looks as if they should have done, sergeant,' commented the captain.

Abandoning the inspection, Cantopher checked his revolver, jumped into a truck and drove off at high speed towards the site of the downed aircraft. He was followed by Allworth, another officer, Lieutenant 'Paddy' Yeardsley, and ten men armed with rifles.

They closed in on the Ju 88 as machine gun fire rang out once more, which could possibly have been the German crew trying to destroy parts of the aircraft.

A later report by Flight-Lieutenant Laurence Irving, a British intelligence officer, refers to a Colonel Macnamara, who, by most accounts, was not present:

The crew of the enemy aircraft got out and opened fire on his platoon with two machine guns and a sub-machine gun. The platoon were preparing to take charge of the aircraft. Colonel Macnamara deployed his men and advanced across 300 yards of absolutely flat country, cut up with dykes.

Soldiers of the London Irish Rifles in 1940, and Ruhlandt's downed Junkers 88, nicknamed 'the Owl'

When they were within 100 yards of the enemy aircraft, the crew waved a white rag. As the troops approached, however, one of them made a dart for the aircraft whereupon the sergeant dashed in, loosing off his revolver. In this melee three of the crew were slightly wounded, but the aircraft was not fired upon.

The troops were within fifty yards of the aircraft when the four Germans surrendered.

Richter recalled: 'During the fighter attack I was wounded in both eyes by glass splinters. Ruhlandt, who was flying his first mission with this crew, was wounded by a shot through the ankle on the ground. The other two crew members remained unwounded.'

More excitable accounts talk of 'the Germans holding out for several hours and taking over a sandbagged gun emplacement' before being detained.

The official report by the MoD's Air Historical Branch, published in 1986, states: 'The crew are also said to have fired at people trying to prevent them from destroying their aircraft and coming to arrest them; this, however, cannot be confirmed and is completely denied by the crew. During this engagement, three of the crew were wounded.'

The report continues: 'It would appear that some sort of fight took place, but it is far from clear that the crew fired at anything but their own aircraft. It may therefore be that to characterise this skirmish as a battle would be something of an exaggeration.'

Some reports suggest, however, that the troops were later repri-manded for opening fire without receiving orders to do so.

Having captured the enemy crew, Cantopher, a bomb-disposal officer who spoke a little German, overheard his prisoners apparently discussing how the aircraft might explode at any moment.

According to the London Irish Regiment, it was originally thought that this might be some sort of 'Teutonic practical joke'. Cantopher was taking no chances, however. Sending his men and their prisoners away, he entered the damaged aircraft, found an explosive charge under one of the wings and threw it into a nearby drainage ditch. His actions preserved the prized aircraft for exam-ination by RAF engineers.

Cantopher was later given the George Medal for 'conspicuous

gallantry in carrying out hazardous work in a very brave manner'; the award was gazetted in the *Supplement to the London Gazette* dated 22 January 1941 and reported in *The Times* the next day.

Two sisters, Sheila Gillham, who was ten at the time, and Brenda Hitches, who was eight, reported that their father, Charles Walden, 'stored the downed bomber in his garage until it could be looked at by air intelligence'.

The aircraft, which had a maximum speed of 292 mph and a range of 1,696 miles, was taken to RAF Farnborough for examination, which revealed highly valuable information – including the presence of a secret and extremely accurate new bombsight.

Richter concluded his report of the incident by writing: 'A detachment of soldiers arrested us and took us into custody, where we were very well treated. After interrogation I was taken to a hospital and operated on in both eyes.'

According to official reports, the prisoners were taken to the London Irish headquarters at Mount Ephraim. Other accounts suggest that there might have been a detour via the Sportsman Inn.

The author of one report said: 'I lunched with the London Irish and later saw the German crew. All except one (a very poor type) were tough enough in the gangster manner.'

In 2010 Corporal George Willis, who had been the regiment's piper and by then was aged ninety, recalled having been at the Sportsman when his comrades returned with their prisoners. 'The men were in good spirits and came into the pub with the Germans,' he said. 'We gave the Germans pints of beer in exchange for a few souvenirs. I got a set of enamel Luftwaffe wings.'

Little is known about Ruhlandt's career before or after the Battle of Graveney Marsh. He was contacted by Saunders in 1987, who was compiling a book, *Images of War: Luftwaffe Bombers in the Battle of Britain.*

Ruhlandt replied: 'My captivity was spent with my comrades in Canada, where I was eventually released on 6 December 1946.'

Saunders added, that the German pilot 'avoided giving any specific detail of the circumstances of his capture'.

In 2010, the seventieth anniversary of the Battle of Graveney Marsh – if indeed such a battle ever took place – was officially commemorated for the first time when sixty members of the London

Irish Rifles Regimental Association attended an unveiling of a plaque at the Sportsman Inn to commemorate the occasion.

Sheila and Brenda, then aged eighty and seventy-eight, attended. 'The service brought back lots of little memories,' Sheila said. 'It was wonderful.'

The incident was featured in *The Forgotten Frontline*, an exhibition at Whitstable Museum illustrating how the Kent coast was affected by the war.

According to Nigel Wilkinson, the vice-chairman of the Whitstable Museum Association: 'Although it barely gets a mention in the history books, Graveney Marsh was the last battle to take place on British soil involving a foreign enemy. At the time the aircraft was a new marque and as it was only two weeks old, it provided the Air Ministry with valuable intelligence. Of course, the men of the London Irish Rifles spoke about the battle. It went down in regimental folklore.'

Andy Saunders remains dubious. He concluded his account of the action by discounting the more fanciful reports of the battle. 'It is not difficult to imagine the scene at the Sportsman Inn that night, where it is more than likely that the enthusiastically celebrating soldiers downed a few pints of Guinness. No doubt, in the telling and retelling of the tales, the events got a little more embellished.'

While the story of the 'Battle of Graveney Marsh' may indeed have read like the script to an episode of *Dad's Army*, the clash is reported in the records of the 1st London Irish Rifles at Kew. They were originally classified until 2042.

The Italian fighter pilot Guiseppe Ruzzin, an optimist with a smile to match, in Spain during the civil war. He escorted bombers of the Regia Aeronautica against targets on England's south coast in 1940

16

Warrant Officer Guiseppe Ruzzin
Fiat CR42 Biplane Fighter

22 October 1940

*For all their limitations, the Italian pilots
were like an aerobatics team.*

THE OMENS FOR the Italian fighter pilot Guiseppe Ruzzin were
not exactly favourable when he arrived at his new base at
Ursel in Belgium with orders to join the German air assault on
Britain.

An optimist with a smile to match, Ruzzin was a young man
with a passion for flying, but he had little reason to be cheerful in
the autumn of 1940: the weather over north-west Europe and the
prospects for his mission were both deteriorating. The Luftwaffe
had already failed to establish aerial superiority over the Channel
and Operation Sealion – the German invasion of Britain – had
been postponed indefinitely.

One other factor counted against Ruzzin and his comrades from
the Corpo Aero Italiano, a force of 180 aircraft later dubbed the
'Chianti Raiders': they were not exactly welcomed by their erstwhile
allies.

Posted to four bases in Belgium, the Italians found that two of
these had, perhaps with a touch of German malice, been codenamed
'Daedalus' (Melsbroek) and 'Icarus' (Chievres) after the two figures
from Greek mythology. Daedalus had constructed a pair of wings
by sticking feathers to a wooden frame with wax. His son Icarus
ignored his father's warnings and flew too close to the sun, which
melted the wax, and he fell to his death in the sea.

For many Italian airmen, the first meetings with their Luftwaffe counterparts were difficult, and not only because of the language barrier. The word 'junk' was used to describe some of the Italian aircraft, with the twin-engine Fiat BR20 bombers being condemned as *pantechnicon*, which translates as 'removal vans'. Some of the Italian airmen were referred to as 'blond arses'. Relations between the ground crews were no better; Luftwaffe technicians resented 'babysitting' the Italians and made their feelings known.

Mussolini had declared war on Britain on 10 June 1940, and his air force had bombed the British naval base on Malta the next day. Just over two weeks later, on 26 June, he had offered to send thirty squadrons north to join the assault on Britain. The offer was rejected.

Hitler and Goering argued that Italian forces were better deployed in the more familiar surroundings of the Mediterranean. Indeed, Luftwaffe commanders warned against sending the Italians to an area where the climate was entirely different from the regions in which they were used to operating – such as Libya and Italian Somaliland – with aircraft that were inferior to those of the RAF's fighter squadrons.

Mussolini persisted, however, and in stronger terms after RAF Bomber Command started targeting Italy's northern cities. In the end, the Italian air force sent a much smaller expeditionary force than envisaged, the Corpo Aero Italiano, which included sixty-six bombers.

The operation did not start well. Seven aircraft were lost because of technical problems on the flights from northern Italy over the Alps to bases in Belgium, where the last elements of the force arrived on 19 October. They were finally declared operational three days later, on 22 October, and told that their targets would be the coastal towns between the mouth of the Thames and the port of Harwich.

Among the Italian airmen destined to fly against these targets on the east coast of England was Ruzzin, now attached to 85 Squadron. He was a veteran of the Spanish Civil War, who had been born in Treviso in the Veneto region of north-east Italy on 25 April 1916, in the shadow of the First World War. Engulfed by that conflict, his family had fled from their home in Spresiano, finding refuge in the port city of Genoa after the Battle of Caporetto, when Italian forces retreated in the face of an Austro-German offensive.

By the age of nineteen, Ruzzin had developed an enthusiasm for flying and, as he said later, he would spend most of the rest of his life 'among aeroplanes'. In 1935 he applied to join the Italian air force, the Regia Aeronautica, gaining his pilot's licence at Calmeri on 25 September, and his military licence at the Aviano military base later that year.

At about the same time, Mussolini pledged support for the nationalist insurgents under Franco in what was to become the Spanish Civil War. After just 110 hours in the air, Ruzzin volunteered to fight in Spain.

Operating under the nom-de-guerre of 'Giacomo Grassi', Ruzzin became the pilot of a highly manoeuvrable Fiat CR32 biplane fighter flying with the 4th Fighter Wing (Gorizia). He scored his first kill – a memorable moment for all fighter pilots – during a patrol over Torrijos, south-west of Madrid, on 7 December 1936, shooting down a single-engine Russian monoplane, a Polikarpov I-16, flying republican colours.

The Polikarpov was a stumpy-looking aircraft, with a huge radial engine and a short fuselage, but the design was considered revolutionary at the time and it could fly 50 mph faster than any other plane in the Spanish conflict. Ruzzin and his nationalist comrades called it the 'Rat'.

According to Peter Haining in his book *The Chianti Raiders*: 'The young Italian took great pride in out-thinking and out-shooting his enemy and seeing him fall in flames on to the scorched terrain of the Iberian Peninsula.'

The identity of the pilot of the Polikarpov is not known, nor whether he survived.

Haining added: 'In the months that followed, Guiseppe Ruzzin earned a notable reputation for his tactics and skill in the aerial warfare that continued over Madrid, Guadalajara, Aragona and Avila. In fourteen months, he spent over 300 hours in the air, took part in 234 missions, and was credited with four kills and six shared destructions.'

On one occasion, when the fifteen aircraft in his unit had been attacked by forty republican 'Rats', Ruzzin crash-landed at an aerodrome at Getalfe with 158 bullet holes in his aircraft. Always romantically minded, he described it as 'a duel' in the skies – 'a game'.

After returning to Italy, Ruzzin worked as an instructor, passing on the lessons he had learnt in Spain. In June 1940, he was based at an aerodrome at Cervere in Piedmont, attacking French airfields in Provence. His aircraft had changed, though; by now he was flying the CR42, nicknamed the 'Falcon'.

While its nickname might have generated images of a sleek, predatory machine, the aircraft was a biplane with an open cockpit and fixed landing gear, which, in 1940, lacked any kind of radio equipment.

Developed by Celestino Rosatelli, an acclaimed Italian aeronautical engineer who worked for Fiat, the CR42 first flew on 23 May 1938. It was compact and highly manoeuvrable.

It replaced the successful CR32, which had also been designed by Rosatelli, but it was considered by many to be a stopgap while the Italian air force awaited the arrival of modern monoplane fighters. The aircraft had a top speed of 275 mph, about 90 mph slower than the Spitfire Mk I, with an air-cooled radial engine. It carried two machine guns, one firing through the propeller. As was often the case with Italian fighters, the aircraft featured a useful counter on the instrument panel for the number of rounds fired. It could also carry 440lb of bombs mounted under the wing when used in a ground-attack role.

When Ruzzin arrived at Ursel in October 1940, the Italians were a source of mirth across the Channel, mocked by cartoonists in British magazines and newspapers. An intelligence report, which was circulated among RAF squadrons, however, warned against complacency, specifically in regard to the biplane fighter.

'The manoeuvrability of the CR42, in particular their capacity to execute an extremely tight roll,' the report said, 'had caused considerable surprise to other pilots and undoubtedly saved many Italian fighters from destruction.' The report added that the aircraft was 'extremely strong'.

The Italian campaign opened on the night of 24 October – the 108th day of the Battle of Britain – with a raid on the port of Harwich, where many naval ships, including destroyers and minesweepers, were moored.

At about 10.30 p.m. residents of the town started to hear the sound of unfamiliar aero engines, like 'rattling tin cans' rather than

Italian airmen with their German allies; a flight of Fiat CR42s

the richer sound of German air power. According to Haining, there was no panic, but everyone headed for the nearest air-raid shelters, and later heard anti-aircraft guns defending the port. The unescorted Italian bombers (BR20s), believed to number sixteen aircraft, flew over the town, however, and dropped their bombs on fields and villages farther inland and along the coast.

By any measure, the raid was a failure. One BR20 crashed on take-off and two crews abandoned their aircraft over the Channel because of a shortage of fuel.

The day after the raid, Field Marshal Erhard Milch, who had overseen the development of the Luftwaffe in the 1930s, asserted that Mussolini's aerial contingent were more of a liability than an asset.

The Italians took a slightly different view. One article in the national press reported: 'A large force of Italian bombers raided London during the night. They have returned bearing the marks of combat, but with the glorious certainty of a great victory.'

In Belgium, Ruzzin prepared to fly his first sortie over Britain. On this occasion the target was another port, Ramsgate, which was a base for motor torpedo boats, known as MTBs.

His logbook states that twelve BR20s accompanied by a dozen biplane fighters crossed the Straits of Dover, which was covered in low cloud, in the late afternoon. The mission was then abandoned because of the lack of visibility.

Three days later, Hitler met Mussolini in Florence. The Italian leader was in confident mood; his forces had that morning invaded Greece, and he told the Fuhrer that it would be all over in a couple of weeks. Hitler later told his closest aides that this was 'madness'; Mussolini should have attacked Malta.

Ruzzin was in the air again on 29 October as part of a much bigger operation against Ramsgate, with fifteen bombers escorted by seventy-three fighters. Three of the bombers turned back because of engine problems, but the rest attacked at low level and dropped seventy-five bombs in the area of Deal.

Five soldiers from the Royal Marines became the first British casualties of the Italian bombing of Britain. Five of the bombers were hit by anti-aircraft fire and several Italian airmen were injured. One died after his parachute failed to open.

The Italians continued to attack British targets until January 1941, when most of the Corpo Aero Italiano returned home. They claimed to have destroyed nine British fighters, but these reports are known to have been exaggerated. Ruzzin is credited with shooting down one Hurricane on 11 November during another raid on Harwich, several days after the official end of the Battle of Britain.

His translated account of the action – the first occasion on which Ruzzin had faced British fighters – is recorded in *The Chianti Raiders*: 'I was near the bombers when the attack developed. I was having trouble with my oxygen. I noted a small convoy of four ships beneath and the next thing to happen was that the British attacked from astern. The melee was fast and furious. I fought against Spitfires and Hurricanes. Gunned 4. Certainly killed one. Landed at St Denis (Ghent).'

In the same air battle, Pilot Officer Edward 'Hawkeye' Wells, a New Zealander, became the first RAF pilot to shoot down an aircraft from the Italian expeditionary force. He acknowledged the acrobatic skills and ingenuity of the Italian pilots, which stood out because of their inferior aircraft, and described one encounter between his Spitfire and the canny pilot of one CR42.

'As I fired,' Wells said, 'he half-rolled very tightly and I was completely unable to hold him, so rapid were his manoeuvres. He immediately disappeared into the cloud sill and was not seen again. I attacked two or three more and fired short bursts, in each case the enemy half-rolled very tightly and easily and completely out-turned me. In two cases, as they came out of their rolls, they were able to turn in almost on my tail and open fire on me.'

For all their limitations, the CR42 pilots were like an aerobatics team. Ruzzin liked what he called the 'purity' of flying the aircraft and the thrill of what he described as 'primitive flying', dismissing the advantages of radio assistance, radar, and computing. It required, he argued, less imagination on the part of the pilot.

Ruzzin went on to fly forty different aircraft, including the Messerschmitt 109, with little training. 'Young men, here you have the new combat machines given by Hitler, now get along and good luck!' is how he recalled his introduction to the German fighter.

The most memorable moment in his long combat career is typical Ruzzin: good-humoured, at ease with himself, a knight of the sky on 29 June 1943, over Sicily. He had engaged in 'vigorous' combat with a British Spitfire, which had attacked the airfield at Comiso. Ruzzin recalled how he took off at 2.30 p.m. under a scorching sun.

Flying in fan-formation, he and his fellow pilots were told by radio of the presence of Allied fighters. Excited, the Italians quickly joined the Me 109s of the German Fontanarossa division; British aircraft shortly filled the air with such frenzy that it 'evolved into a disordered carousel, similar to a swarm of angry wasps'.

While attempting to attack a Spitfire, Ruzzin briefly lost control of his aircraft and then found himself being swiftly pursued by the enemy. He resorted to a desperate manoeuvre that had saved his life in the past: 'a high-speed stall with autorotation'. After a brief loss of altitude, he recovered, and the two aircraft engaged in 'incessant acrobatics'.

In Ruzzin's words: 'The game now had a rule and the duel had to commit us to its epilogue . . . I will never know how long this death carousel lasted. The space below us became thinner and thinner. Then, only the hard earth. But something happened in the last phase: I managed to gain an angle from which to try the last chance . . . I pressed the weapons button . . . nothing. Not one shot left, I had finished the ammunition.

'Then I saw the Spitfire continue straight ahead, gaining altitude without more manoeuvring. Instinctively, I thought he too was in my same condition. Now we were no longer adversaries, but only two aviators. I approached cautiously, until I brought the end of my left wing almost in contact with his. He did not disappear. All this, as if it were a normal exercise of acrobatic peacetime patrol. We looked at each other and we felt the desire to see each other face to face.

'We both took off our oxygen masks and pulled back the goggles. Now we saw each other perfectly: I had a dark moustache, he [had] the soft moustache, with the tips down, blond, typical of the English sportsman.

'We both greeted each other in the most natural way with a wave of our hand. Then we "broke" the singular couple; with a turn to the left he headed for Malta, while I . . . pointed to the field of Comiso already in sight.

'In the few minutes that preceded the landing I felt a sense of unutterable joy, I took a deep breath and invaded an intense satisfaction, the same that the honest man feels after doing a good deed.'

Three hours later, Ruzzin was back in combat. The frank, but lyrical, slightly wistful style of recollection is typical of Ruzzin's almost romanticised depiction of aviation.

He was still contemplating his war record a few days before his death. In a distinguished career over forty years, Ruzzin flew 433 combat missions. He was credited with five enemy aircraft destroyed and several damaged, and was decorated with four Italian military medals for valour, as well as the German Iron Cross, 2nd class.

In the postwar period, he remained with the Italian air force and reached the rank of brigadier general, accumulating more than 3,500 flying hours and lending his expertise to a new generation of pilots. Ruzzin died in 2009, aged ninety-two.

His protégé, the leading Italian ace Luigi Gorrini, campaigned long after the war for greater recognition for the Italians who fought in the Battle of Britain, but the history books have not been kind to the Chianti Raiders.

According to historians at the RAF Museum at Hendon, north London: 'The Italians shot down no RAF aircraft – despite numerous claims – but lost two dozen [aircraft] in a rather ineffectual campaign that caused little damage, having suffered from limited experience and training, using outdated aircraft and tactics.'

After months in which the RAF had been unable to defend the country against night bombing, it now had a truly aggressive weapon – the Beaufighter would go on to become one of the most formidable aircraft of the Second World War

17

Sergeant Arthur Hodgkinson
Mk 1F Bristol Beaufighter
Twin-Engine Heavy Fighter

25 October 1940

It was known as the '10-gun terror'.
To many of its crews, it was simply the 'Beau'.

L IKE CHARACTERS FROM a 1930s horror film, Arthur Hodgkinson and his crewman Bertram Dye stalked their prey in the hours of darkness and, in the manner of an Ealing Studios production, became known as the 'Night Twins'.

With the aid of a powerful new aircraft that could 'see in the dark' – the twin-engine Bristol Beaufighter equipped with airborne radar – the two sergeants started to find and destroy enemy bombers just as the terror of the Blitz was gripping Britain. Up to this point, the RAF had been virtually impotent against the German night bomber, but this was about to change.

On the evening of 25 October, Hodgkinson followed an enemy aircraft while guided by Dye, who was operating the new tracking equipment then known as Airborne Interception or AI. The catchy American word 'radar' gained currency later.

While a waning crescent moon hung over the night, barely touching the darkness, the British pilot found the German bomber at 16,000ft. He later recorded events.

'I was vectored out 170 degrees and back 350 degrees on to [the] enemy aircraft . . . and observed the enemy flying slightly to my north side ahead of me at a distance of 400 yards,' Hodgkinson recalled in the combat report filed with 219 Squadron, based at

Redhill aerodrome in Surrey. He had been flying in the area of Kenley, thirteen miles south of central London. It was about 7 p.m., a day after British summer time had been extended throughout the autumn and winter.

As Hodgkinson closed in on his target, he 'opened fire at 200 yards – firing approximately 150 rounds in two bursts. I gave a third burst at 70 yards but the cannons failed to fire.'

His report continued:

> My AI operator, Sgt Dye, observed the enemy aircraft dive steeply into cloud. E/a [enemy aircraft] returned no fire. The aircraft was definitely a Do 17 or Do 215. I noticed the humped effect above forward end of fuselage (where the aerial is) and high wing, also twin rudders.

The report was signed A.J. Hodgkinson, with a big lower case 'a' for a capital letter, in his neat rightward slanting hand. For Hodgkinson, who was nicknamed 'Hodge' and had been in action throughout the Battle of Britain, it was a memorable night; this was his first kill.

When he was awarded the Distinguished Flying Cross a few months later, the citation, published in the *London Gazette* on 11 April 1941, read: 'His eagerness to seek and destroy the enemy at night has set a splendid example to his fellow pilots.'

The date of 25 October 1940 also marked the first occasion on which the new Beaufighter had successfully shot down an enemy aircraft. This was auspicious. After months in which the RAF had been unable to defend the country against night bombing, the service now had a truly aggressive weapon – and the Beaufighter would go on to become one of the most formidable aircraft of the Second World War.

Its emergence also marked a triumph for British aeronautical enterprise. In the years immediately before the war, the Bristol Aircraft Company had recognised the need for a high-performance long-range fighter, and then developed the Beaufighter as a company project independent of the government and official specifications dictated by the Air Ministry. Two qualities marked out the aircraft: its speed and firepower.

The plane flown by Hodgkinson on 25 October had two enormous supercharged Bristol Hercules radial engines and could reach
323 mph at 15,000ft, with a range of 1,500 miles. Its firepower
included four 20mm cannon and six machine guns. A single burst
from the cannon was often enough to destroy a German bomber.
To some the aircraft was known as the '10-gun terror'. To many
of its crews, it was simply the 'Beau'.

One famous crewman, Jimmy Rawnsley, described his first sight
of the aircraft in the autumn of 1940 in his memoir, *Night Fighter*.
'There she stood, sturdy, powerful, fearsome, surrounded by an
enthusiastic crowd,' Rawnsley wrote. Once inside, he noted: 'It was
dim in the tunnel-like fuselage, but as my eyes became accustomed
to the half-light I saw them, two on each side of the catwalk: four
solid great cannon, firmly set in place just below floor level. Their
massive breaches gleamed with an evil beauty.'

After flying in Bristol Blenheims as an air gunner with 604
Squadron, Rawnsley had to retrain as a radar operator, which
demanded great skill. In his book, he recalled a memorable lecture
delivered by a young radar specialist, Donald Parry, who made the
science sound simple.

Rawnsley wrote: 'Inside the improvised lecture room, with the
doors locked, we took our places on wooden benches. I had that
tense, expectant feeling that comes over one on entering a strange
country for the first time.

'"AI," Parry said, "works on the same principle as an ordinary
sound echo. You shout 'Boo' across a valley, and after a short interval
the echo shouts 'Boo' back at you. You time the interval, and
knowing the speed of sound you can work out the distance across
the valley."

'Pausing to let that sink in, Parry then went on: "Now if you
use some sort of directional ear-trumpet, like a sound locator, you
can tell the direction from which the 'boo' is coming."'

Rawnsley added: 'There were grins of relief going round the
room, along with eager demonstrations of imaginary ear-trumpets.
It was not going to be such heavy going as we had feared.

'"All that AI does, then," the lecturer went on, "is to send out a
series of radio 'Boos'. If there is another aircraft within range, an
echo bounces back from it, and the AI tells you its range and bearing."'

A gregarious man renowned for his sense of humour, Rawnsley was an enthusiastic champion of airborne radar, and made his name flying with John Cunningham, the most famous British night-fighter pilot of all. Cunningham's success – he destroyed twenty enemy aircraft – was put down to a hearty consumption of carrots, which were said to sharpen his eyesight, and gave rise to the nickname 'Cat's Eyes' Cunningham.

While Hodgkinson would also rank among the leading night-fighter aces, he did not enjoy the same public profile as Cunningham, who had been educated at Whitgift, a private school in Croydon, and later became a leading test pilot. Hodgkinson never wrote a memoir, and no record appears to exist of his opinion of the Beaufighter or airborne radar, but he made highly effective use of both. He was a quieter kind of killer.

A photograph of him on the Battle of Britain London Monument website shows him sitting cross-legged, his hands clasped, looking straight at the camera. With his head slanted slightly to his left, his thin lips closed, and hooded eyes, Hodgkinson gives the air of a quietly determined man.

He was born Arthur John Hodgkinson in Calcutta, British India, on August 31, 1915, the third of the five children of William Hodgkinson and his wife, Louise Amy. Always known in the family as 'Jack', he had two brothers and two sisters. His elder brother, Billy, also joined the RAF, but was killed in a flying accident at Cranwell in 1930.

Jack's father was an electrical engineer and inventor who had moved to India at the turn of the century and worked on the first hydro-electric projects on the subcontinent. William Hodgkinson later became relatively wealthy because of an invention – related to radar – called The Marine Direction Finder, which detected merchant ships crossing the Atlantic. He fell ill in 1924 and returned to Britain a year later after a long stay in Switzerland.

His middle son was a bright boy who won a place at Amersham Grammar School in Buckinghamshire. In January 1932, at the age of sixteen, Jack Hodgkinson joined the RAF as an aircraft appren-tice as part of the twenty-fifth intake at the No. 1 School of Technical Training at Halton, Buckinghamshire, established in 1919. The school had a reputation for engineering excellence, strict discipline, and engendering a robust spirit among the thousands of boys, many from working-class backgrounds, who would form the skilled ground crews essential to the maintenance of the RAF during the Second World War. It also gave many the chance to fly.

As with Nelson's navy more than a century before, the increasingly meritocratic nature of the RAF at this time was found in the training school, which held entrance exams around the country. Not everyone approved. In a Commons debate in 1926, one MP, Sir Frank Nelson, complained that the cost of training an apprentice, then about £230 a year (£14,000 today), was 'probably more than it costs a parent to send a boy to any of the four or five leading public schools of England'.

The nature of discipline at Halton also raised some eyebrows, not least among the boys, who were widely known as 'brats'.

As one former trainee, Group Captain Min Larkin, noted: 'Each apprentice was issued with a small booklet entitled *Standing Orders for Apprentices*. This contained a myriad of rules which severely restricted an apprentice's freedom to spend what precious spare time he was allowed as he might wish. "These rules are necessary for your own benefit," apprentices were often told by their superiors . . . "Apprentices are to take a bath twice a week" and "Apprentices are prohibited from visiting public houses and consuming alcohol."

'One of the oddest rules was: "Females are not to attend the monthly Apprentice dances." Perhaps the most resented rule, especially by older apprentices in their third year of training, was lights out by 21.45, when their former school chums were still out enjoying themselves with their girlfriends.'

At the same time, recreational opportunities were abundant, including a wide range of sports facilities, and medical and dental care were among the best in the country. Hodgkinson played rugby and tennis and was a good cross-country runner.

Most apprentices regarded it as a point of honour to break as many of the rules as possible. Indeed, at Halton the 'air force spirit' grew and Hodgkinson flourished. He passed out in December 1934 as Fitter, Aero Engines, and later successfully applied for pilot training. He later served with 70 Squadron at RAF Habbaniya in Iraq, flying Vickers Valentia transport aircraft. According to letters home at the time, he enjoyed horse riding and visiting the al-Rashid cinema in Baghdad, where he watched *David Copperfield* starring WC Fields.

By June 1940, on the eve of the Battle of Britain, he was flying with 219 Squadron, which was a night-fighter unit equipped with twin-engine Bristol Blenheims. Flying at night was a dangerous and unpredictable business in those days, when aircraft had few of the technical aids that would help crews later in the war. Many perished in the darkness because of simple navigational errors and other mishaps.

Hodgkinson thrived, however, and it was not long before the twenty-four-year-old was confronting the enemy in the Battle of Britain at the start of an eventful combat career as a fighter pilot.

During the night of 21 July, he attacked an unidentified enemy aircraft at 3.25 a.m. According to his combat report, he was flying 'near some searchlight intersections near Leeds', when his air gunner saw the enemy 'pass to our left and fired two bursts'.

On 5 August, he wrecked the undercarriage of his Blenheim while taking off and was later forced to crash-land with his wheels up. He escaped without injury.

Then came the momentous events of 15 August, later known as 'Black Thursday' by the Luftwaffe because of its heavy losses. On that day, the German air force launched its only significant daylight raids on the north of England, from bases in Scandinavia.

Hodgkinson was flying one of eleven aircraft from 219 Squadron, which were scrambled to confront an enemy formation of Junkers 88s heading for Scarborough in North Yorkshire. As the battle unfolded, the Blenheims were joined by Spitfires from 616 Squadron, Hurricanes from 73 Squadron and Defiants from 264 Squadron. The weather conditions were good with unlimited visibility.

As the Blenheims approached the enemy force, they broke formation and attacked fifteen German bombers near Flamborough.

Flying in 'Red Section', Hodgkinson followed Red Leader from 13,000ft to 7,000ft in pursuit of several enemy aircraft. He told intelligence officers later that he 'saw a Ju 88 on my left, which I first thought was a Blenheim till I noticed the black cross on the fuselage. I made a quarter attack.' Black smoke emerged from the German bomber after Hodgkinson's first burst of fire, but the Ju 88 increased speed and drew away, increasing the range from 150 yards to about 350 yards.

Hogkinson then 'fired off all my ammunition in bursts from astern, above and below and could see the smoke of the incendiaries entering the aircraft, but the enemy failed to come down. No fire noticed from rear gunner. 2,300 rounds fired.'

While the pilots of 219 Squadron were often seen chasing Ju 88s far out to sea, they claimed to have damaged nine enemy aircraft.

One Blenheim with wounded crew crash-landed at the aerodrome at Driffield, which had been attacked by the Luftwaffe. Five hangars were hit and fourteen British service personnel perished, including nineteen-year-old Margueritte Hudson, the first member of the WAAF to be killed during the summer of 1940.

Hodgkinson waited another eight weeks for the arrival of the vaunted Beaufighter before he could claim his first confirmed kill, but the outcome of the Battle of Britain was not in doubt by the time he took off from Redhill on the night of 25 October 1940.

By then some of the most destructive infighting was taking place within the ranks of the RAF's senior commanders. Air Vice-Marshal Keith Park, head of 11 Group, which defended London and the Southeast, and Air Vice-Marshal Trafford Leigh-Mallory, head of 12 Group in the Midlands, were still clashing over tactics. Park had always husbanded his resources, using his squadrons in small groups, harrying the Germans wherever and whenever they appeared; Leigh-Mallory advocated the 'Big Wing strategy' in which dozens of aircraft attacked the Luftwaffe at the same time.

While Air Chief Marshal Sir Hugh Dowding tried to pacify the two men, his time as head of Fighter Command was coming to an end. The victor of the Battle of Britain would be one of its greatest casualties, an enigmatic man who had saved his country from the Nazi threat, but who was largely unloved by his ungrateful contemporaries at the Air Ministry.

As Dowding struggled for survival, the Luftwaffe ranged across Britain once again, after a period in which the weather had restricted flying. On 25 October, they bombed London, using high-flying fighter bombers; they also hit Liverpool and Cardiff, mined waters off north-east Scotland, East Anglia and Merseyside, and sank the South Goodwin Lightship off St Margaret's Bay, Kent. The Luftwaffe lost fifteen aircraft; the RAF lost ten.

On the same day, Bomber Command launched raids against the

German coastal cities of Hamburg and Kiel. Several fires were reported across Hamburg, where three people were killed and twenty injured.

In the wider war, Philippe Pétain, the leader of Vichy France, met Hitler at Montoire-sur-le-Loir, where he turned down the Fuhrer's request to bring his regime into the war on Germany's side. He did, however, agree to collaborate with the Axis powers. And in a sign of a conflict to come, Japanese naval aircraft bombed Chungking (narrowly missing the American embassy), which then served as the capital of China.

After destroying the German intruder over Surrey, Hodgkinson and Dye continued to work up their skills on the Beaufighter and its new equipment.

By the spring of 1941, they had shot down three enemy aircraft and damaged several more, with Hodgkinson promoted to pilot officer. His combat report for 13 March 1941 includes a graphic account of the destruction of a Dornier 17 near Winchester. On this occasion he was guided by ground controllers, because the elevation tube on his AI set was faulty and Dye was unable to fix it while airborne.

The account gives the reader a clear picture of what it was like 'hunting' in the skies over southern England at night.

He wrote (in short, almost staccato sentences, with little punctuation):

Overshot and turned round to starboard on to 340 degrees again making contact [with the enemy bomber] and again coming up at 180 mph into minimum range and overshooting – moon behind us and dark layer to north below and fairly light sky above horizon.

Handed over to Beetle [ground controllers at Tangmere aerodrome in Sussex] – vectored back to base – sent out on 170 degrees – handed over to Flintlock [ground controllers at Durrington in Wiltshire], vectored 180 degrees turned port on to 340 degrees at 20,000 feet made contact, overshot again passed minimum range having lost height to 14,000 feet.

Turned to port put on 20 degrees of flap went into fine pitch and came up again on 340 degrees, and made contact. Told to turn port, lose height, steady, turned on to 340 degrees and came

up on to bandit slowly from 3,000 feet behind saw black silhou-
ette below and to port, slid down behind, opened up and fired
from 100 yards behind.

After a two-second burst my nose dropped slightly, so stopped
firing and saw flashes appear on enemy aircraft. Starboard engine
caught fire and e/a did shallow dive to port. Gave another
two-second burst and e/a dived steeply to earth with a red glow
and burst into flames on striking the ground.

The identities of the four men who flew in the Dornier are not
known.

On that night and the next, 1,200 people died and more than
1,000 were seriously injured as 400 bombers attacked the shipbuilding
yards and related industries on Clydeside. Of the 12,000 houses in
Clydebank, only eight were undamaged. The town was evacuated.

While Britain's defences remained inadequate at night, the
Beaufighter was beginning to appear in larger numbers. In a letter
to his sister Betty on 17 March, 1941, Hodgkinson wrote: 'Our
Beaufighters have suddenly jumped into the news – we've had quite
a few "squirts" in the last week and on Thursday night got 4 destroyed,
one probable and one damaged. I got a Heinkel which went straight
into the deck and burst into flames. It was a good sight and I'm
afraid I felt no compunction about it whatever.

By the end of June, 'Hodge' had joined the list of RAF aces as
the reputation of the 'Night Twins' grew. Official recognition came,
too; Hodgkinson was awarded a Bar to his DFC, which was
gazetted on 6 June 1941, while Dye was awarded a Bar to his
Distinguished Flying Medal. The joint citation stated: 'Both have
displayed exceptional skill and keenness which, combined with
excellent teamwork, has resulted in the destruction of at least six
enemy aircraft at night.'

A press cutting referring to the two men as the 'Night Twins'
shows them after the announcement: Dye beams at the camera,
while Hodgkinson reveals just a hint of a smile.

By the end of July, Hodgkinson's tally was nine enemy aircraft
destroyed. He was then 'rested' until March 1942, when he teamed
up again with Dye. They were part of a new unit with new aircraft
– in 264 Squadron flying the twin-engine, multi-role Mosquito,

*Arthur Hodgkinson, front row, third left, in front of one of
No 219 Squadron's Blenheim's; and the 'Night Twins' in 1940*

Pilot - Officer
A. J. Hodgkin-
son (right),
and Sgt. B. E.
D y e, the
"Night Twins."
They won the
D.F.C. and
D.F.M. to-
gether; now
they've won a
bar to each.

another formidable aircraft – on their second tour of operations, based at Colerne in north Wiltshire.

They attacked and damaged a Dornier 217 south-east of Portland Bill on the night of 28 June 1942, but otherwise this was a relatively uneventful period in Hodgkinson's combat career; the bulk of the Luftwaffe was otherwise engaged in Russia.

In February 1943, Hodgkinson was promoted to flight lieutenant and posted to the Middle East, where he joined 23 Squadron, flying Mosquitos out of RAF Luqa on Malta. No documents or letters appear to exist that give any insights into Hodgkinson's state of mind at this time. After three years of almost continuous aerial combat, he was a celebrated RAF veteran, still single, and still eager to fly.

He was in action throughout the next six months, as the Allies prepared for the invasion of Sicily after the defeat of German forces in North Africa.

At 7.35 p.m. on 23 March 1943, he was on a train-busting mission over western Sicily when his navigator, Warrant Officer William Woodman, was hit in the head by a stray .303 bullet. Woodman, who came from Haltwhistle in Northumberland, was twenty-five, two years younger than 'Hodge'. He is buried in the Kalcara naval cemetery on Malta: plot E, grave 05.

There was no let-up in operations. On July 10 – the day the Allies invaded Sicily – Hodgkinson was flying in support of the landings, but failed to return from a low-level attack on railways near Rome. His aircraft, HJ740, hit high-tension cables and crashed on a racecourse. He is buried with his navigator, Sergeant Vincent Crapper, in the Beach Head War Cemetery at Anzio on the west coast of Italy. Hodgkinson was twenty-seven. Crapper, who came from Old Trafford in Manchester, was twenty-two.

Six weeks later, Hodgkinson's 'Night Twin', Bertram Dye, was also killed. Flying in a Beaufighter with 96 Squadron, Dye lost his life at 10.30 p.m. on 31 August 1943, when his aircraft collided with an American B17 bomber, which was on a training flight over Norfolk. Dye is buried in St Peter's New Burial Ground in Bedlington, near his home in Northumberland. He was twenty-two.

The pilot of the Beaufighter, Flying Officer Frederick Robertson DFM, also died in the accident. Another veteran of the Battle of

Britain, Robertson was an RAF ace with twelve kills. He was twenty-five. Nine members of the American crew, who flew with the 305th Bombardment Group, 422 Bomb Squadron, also perished that night.

Two weeks after his death, Hodgkinson was awarded the Distinguished Service Order (DSO), which is given for gallantry on active operations, and is regarded as just short of a Victoria Cross.

The citation read:

This officer has completed much operational flying. Latterly in the Middle East, he has bombed targets in Tunisia, Italy and Sicily and, during these operations, he has attacked numerous locomotives to good effect, while fires have been started in railway installations and sidings as a result of his determined work.

In addition, Flight Lieutenant Hodgkinson has executed many sorties over enemy airfields during which he has destroyed three hostile aircraft and caused much disorganisation. His sterling work has contributed in a large measure to the success of his squadron.

Bernhard Jope was the pilot of a Focke-Wulf Condor, an elegant four-engine maritime bomber that could range over the Atlantic and act as the eyes of German submarines hunting Allied convoys

18

Lieutenant Bernhard Jope
Focke-Wulf 200 Condor
Four-Engine Maritime Bomber

10 July – 31 October 1940

*Although he had not done enough to sink
the Empress of Britain, her fate was sealed.*

THE GERMAN AIR assault in the summer and autumn of 1940
was only one element of a three-pronged campaign aimed at
defeating Britain in the year after the French surrender.

While it involved the bombers and fighters of the Luftwaffe as
the main offensive weapon in the Battle of Britain, it also involved
diplomatic manoeuvres and a blockade, which was put in place by
the German navy, particularly its submarines, known as U-boats, with
support from the air. This became known as the Battle of the
Atlantic, which lasted from September 1939 to May 1945.

In the diplomatic field, Hitler tried to persuade his fellow
European dictators – Mussolini, who had established fascism in Italy;
Franco, who had emerged as the victor of Spain's civil war with
significant German military help; and Pétain, the head of Vichy
France – to exert pressure on Britain.

None of the three wanted to be regarded as subordinate to the
Fuhrer. Mussolini was bent on following his own path in North
Africa and the Balkans, with disastrous long-term consequences for
the Germans, who would be drawn into campaigns that later depleted
their forces in Russia.

Franco refused to commit his impoverished country to fighting
on the German side, with the result that Hitler was never able to

occupy Gibraltar, which would become a decisive British asset in the war in North Africa and the Battle of the Atlantic. The administration of Pétain, meanwhile, which loathed the British, broke off diplomatic relations but refused to declare war on France's one-time ally.

Hitler was always in two minds about his relationship with London and indecisive about the best way to achieve his aims. On the one hand he was at war with Britain, but what he really wanted was peace with Churchill's government, as the British historian A.J.P. Taylor explained in his 1974 book, *The Second World War: An Illustrated History*.

'This would actually transform her [Britain] into a buffer against an American attack,' wrote Taylor. 'All danger on Germany's Western Front would be removed and Hitler would be free to turn against Soviet Russia. But he had only one tactic with which to create a situation favourable to himself: to wait until his opponent's nerve cracked.

'He had followed this tactic before he became Chancellor in Germany,' added Taylor. 'He had followed it with Czechoslovakia and tried to follow it with Poland. He followed it now with Great Britain. During the armistice negotiations with the French, Hitler said: "The British have lost the war, but they don't know it; one must give them time, and they will come round."'

But the British did not crack – nor did they come round. Unlike Hitler's friends in Europe, Britain's allies rallied to the cause of the so-called Mother Country. The Canadians supplied Britain's military needs on generous terms, and with their fellow dominions, South Africa, Australia and New Zealand, sent men and women to fight and support operations on land, on sea and in the air. The key to their involvement – and, indeed, the outcome of the war – was keeping the shipping lanes open.

As the Battle of Britain was being played out in the skies over southern England, the Germans exerted further pressure from their newly won submarine bases on the west coast of France. They called this period *Die Gluckliche Zeit* – 'The Happy Time' – with good reason: they sank nearly 300 Allied ships.

In September 1940, the U-boats started to hunt in packs with great impact: on the twenty-first of that month, Allied ships sailing as 'Convoy HX72' – forty-two vessels – were attacked by four German submarines, with eleven ships sunk and two damaged over two nights. Mussolini then sent twenty-seven Italian submarines to join the campaign in the Atlantic.

On the surface, German raiders such as the battleships *Scharnhorst* and *Gneisenau* ranged across the Atlantic. At the same time, a department of German naval intelligence – known as B-Dienst – cracked British naval codes.

And in the air, pilots such as Bernhard Jope, flying long-range Focke-Wulf 200 Condors, acted as the eyes of the U-boat fleet, reporting on the positions of convoys and bombing Allied shipping that was sailing beyond its own air cover. It was at this moment that Britain was in the greatest peril.

Jope was an experienced German pilot who flew missions from Bordeaux across the Bay of Biscay, the eastern Atlantic and the North Sea throughout the duration of the Battle of Britain, in a plane that had been built as an airliner. It is one of the more remarkable examples of a machine conceived in peacetime that was radically reworked to become an offensive weapon in time of war.

The Condor was designed by Ludwig Mittelhube and built by the Focke-Wulf company based in Bremen. At the time, the four-engine Condor was the most modern airliner in existence and it owed its name to its large 33m wingspan. It made its first test flight in July 1937.

The original specification was for a passenger plane that could accommodate twenty-six people in two cabins in an all-metal airframe designed to fly a little under 10,000ft. This was the limit for a non-pressurised cabin.

In peacetime, the Condor was intended to fly passengers across the Atlantic from Europe to the USA and in 1938 it became the first land-based aircraft to fly non-stop between Berlin and New York. In 1939, Joachim von Ribbentrop, the German Foreign Minister, flew in a Condor to sign the German–Soviet Non-Aggression Pact in Moscow.

As war approached, the aircraft was quickly modified after the Japanese Navy ordered a military version for search and patrol duties. None was delivered to Tokyo, but these planes became the basis for the Condors used by the Luftwaffe for long-range reconnaissance and maritime bombing. The Luftwaffe also used them throughout the Second World War as transport planes and they were used during the siege of Stalingrad to drop supplies to the beleaguered Sixth Army in late 1942.

The military version of the Condor was the biggest aircraft in the Luftwaffe's inventory. It could carry bombs or anti-shipping mines under its wings and it had four gun positions in the fuselage, two on the top and two beneath the cockpit.

However, because the original airframe design had never been intended for use in combat, the stresses of aerial manoeuvres under attack, plus the extra weight of guns and munitions, caused structural failures. At least eight Condors were lost when the fuselage collapsed on landing. A variant was introduced in 1941 that featured a strengthened airframe to prevent further losses.

Hitler used one early Condor – without any armaments – as his personal aircraft. This plane was reconfigured as a two-cabin airliner with comfortable seating for the German leader, who worked at a varnished wooden table with an oxygen set stored within easy reach in case of emergency. Photographs of the aircraft show an airspeed indicator, an altimeter and what appears to be a radio compass and clock mounted on the bulkhead near where Hitler sat.

The plane was named 'Immelmann III' in honour of Max Immelmann, a First World War flying ace. It was destroyed at Berlin Tempelhof airport during an Allied bombing raid in July 1944.

During the Battle of Britain and as the Battle of the Atlantic intensified, the Condor became a reconnaissance aircraft for the Luftwaffe, harrying Britain's supply lines. Churchill recognised its usefulness to the Germans, describing the plane as a 'formidable' partner to the U-boat menace. It was in October 1940 that Jope – then with the rank of lieutenant – used the plane to disable the Canadian Pacific cruise liner *Empress of Britain*, which was subsequently sunk by a U-boat while under tow. She was the largest civilian ship lost in the war.

The *Empress of Britain* had been one of the fastest and most luxurious liners in the world, as she plied her trade between Southampton and Canada during the 1930s. The 42,500-ton ship with three identical funnels on a 720ft hull carried a crew of more than 400 and could accommodate more than 1,000 passengers. She

Jope, left, saluting his commander after bombing the great liner Empress of Britain in 1940

Jope, hands on hips, after the raid; a Condor in flight

was capable of a top speed in excess of 25 knots and had been built robustly in steel to protect her hull from the danger of icebergs.

One of her last voyages before the outbreak of war was a trip from Halifax, Nova Scotia to Southampton, ferrying King George VI and Queen Elizabeth home at the end of their royal tour of Canada in June 1939.

As war approached, the great liner was requisitioned as a troopship and painted grey. Among other modifications, anti-aircraft guns were installed on her decks. She then began a series of voyages moving Canadian troops across the Atlantic or transporting soldiers out to Suez via Cape Town. On 26 October, she was underway about 160 miles from the north-west tip of Ireland, when Jope spotted the liner from the cockpit of his Condor on an overcast morning.

What happened next was captured in a vivid account in the *Liverpool Daily Post* three days later. Jope's aircraft entered into 'a deep dive, dropping its bombs and raking the deck with machine gun fire, very soon the vessel was an inferno,' the paper reported:

James Dean of St Andrews St, Edge Hill, Liverpool, said he was below when the bombing started and rushed on deck to see the bomber flying low over the ship. Despite the ruthless machine gun fire and the raging flames along the whole of the deck, there was no panic. An anti-aircraft gun was put out of action, so the ship was unable to reply effectively.

[Dean] feared some were trapped below deck; he got away in a lifeboat and was picked up by a rescue vessel. A steward said a single enemy plane suddenly came out of the clouds, machine gunning the decks and crew as it went. Some bombs dropped wide of the mark and the plane continued to circle the ship before dropping bombs that set the deck ablaze.

'It was like an inferno. Although I have been on the ship for a long time and know every exit from the kitchen, I could not find my way out. All the staircases were ablaze. My only means of escape was through a porthole which I scrambled through and flung myself into the sea.

'The water was icy cold and I kept swimming to prevent myself from becoming frozen. There was a heavy sea and it was impossible to reach the boats against the swell, while those in the boats were unable to pull members of the crew any distance away in the water. I and a colleague who followed me through the porthole, were in the water nearly an hour before we were picked up.'

Among the rescue vessels were two warships and three trawlers, who quickly answered the vessel's SOS. Another survivor said there was no panic, the bombing was over in less than half an hour . . . and many of the crew were unable to escape for some hours, but conducted themselves with exemplary coolness and obeyed orders, despite the rapid extension of the flames and the bursting of ammunition.

Jope was decorated with the Knight's Cross of the Iron Cross for his actions that day. Although he had not done enough to sink the *Empress of Britain*, his report of the ship's whereabouts alerted the German U-boat fleet and her fate was sealed.

Initially Captain Sapworth gave the order to evacuate the burning hulk and most of the crew and 205 passengers were picked up by the destroyers HMS *Echo* and ORP *Burza* (of the Polish navy) and the anti-submarine trawler, HMS *Cape Arcona*. The *Liverpool Daily Post* reported that forty-five people were still listed as missing three days after Jope's attack.

The British Admiralty was determined that the *Empress of Britain* should be salvaged and within twenty-four hours of the attack, the hull was taken under tow by the tugs HMS *Marauder* and HMS *Thames*. She was then taken towards the shore at four knots with air cover from Sunderland flying boats during daylight.

At the same time the German submarine *U-32*, commanded by Hans Jenisch, had located the ships and, although he had to dive to avoid the attention of the Sunderlands and British destroyers, he was able to position himself between them and the liner. Jenisch fired two torpedoes. One detonated prematurely, the second caused a huge explosion. Then he fired again and the liner began to list, before she sank at a position north-west of Bloody Foreland, off the coast of County Donegal.

Rumours circulated that the ship may have been carrying gold as Britain sought to pay for its war effort by shipping bullion to

America from mines in South Africa, from where the *Empress of Britain* had set sail. There were sketchy reports of a salvage effort over the wreck in 1949, but little else was known until 1995, when divers found the empty hull of the ship lying upside down on the seabed.

The bullion room was still intact, however. The divers found no gold, only the skeleton of a person who may have died at the time of the original attack or subsequent sinking, or perhaps may have been trapped during the 1949 salvage effort.

In only one sortie, Bernhard Jope had inflicted huge damage on Allied shipping.

Born in May 1914, Jope joined the Luftwaffe in April 1935. He was a graduate of the technical university in Danzig, where he studied aircraft construction and, by the time he signed up, he had almost completed his flying training at the German Air Transport School.

He flew during the Spanish Civil War – and was awarded the Spanish Cross in Bronze with Swords – and then during the invasion of Poland, before being posted to the maritime patrol unit at Bordeaux known as KG40.

He was taken off operations in November 1942 after the death of two brothers, but a year later he resumed his role as the scourge of shipping, when he led a successful attack on the Italian battle fleet that was en route to Malta to surrender to the Allies.

At the controls of a Dornier 217 bomber equipped with radio-controlled glide bombs, Jope led eleven planes in September 1943 in an operation that sank the Italian battleship *Roma* and seriously damaged her sistership, *Italia*. He later used glide bombs against the battleship HMS *Warspite* off Salerno and the cruisers HMS *Uganda* and USS *Savannah*. All three ships suffered direct hits, but none sank.

In all, 276 Condors were built in three variants between 1937 and 1944, but production never kept up with wartime demands in the face of considerable losses. The aircraft was withdrawn from offensive operations in 1942.

One Condor named *Dania* was seized in Britain after Denmark was invaded by Germany in 1940. The plane was renamed *Wolf* and was initially used by the British Overseas Airways Corporation

(BOAC) for short-haul freight assignments. In 1941, it was handed over to the RAF for use as a trainer for crews learning on four-engine aircraft, but maintenance issues proved too challenging for it to be put into service.

There are no Condors still flying, but a group of German volunteers has been painstakingly restoring the last plane still in existence as a museum piece. This aircraft had ditched in a Norwegian fjord due to technical failure in February 1942. The wreck was recovered in pieces in 1999. It is being rebuilt at the Airbus factory in Bremen with the aim of putting the aircraft on display at the German Museum of Technology in Berlin.

As for Jope, he spent some time in prison at the end of the war, but then joined the German airline Lufthansa, where he worked as a pilot until retirement. He died in July 1995 in Koenigstein aged eighty-one, nearly fifty-five years after the Battle of Britain came to a close. The Blitz and the Battle of the Atlantic grew in intensity, however, and the world moved on to a wider war.

Bibliography

Addison, Paul and Crang, Jeremy A., *The Burning Blue*, Pimlico, 2000

Arthur, Max, *Last of the Few*, Virgin Books, 2011

Beaver, Paul, *Forgotten Few: Naval Fighter Pilots in the Battle of Britain*, Beaver Westminster, 2019

Bekker, Cajus, *The Luftwaffe War Diaries*, Corgi, 1964

Bird, Andrew D., *Coastal Dawn: Blenheims in Action from the Phoney War through the Battle of Britain*, Grub Street Publishing, 2012

Bishop, Edward, *The Daily Telegraph Book of Airmen's Obituaries*, Bounty Books, 2007

Brickhill, Paul, *The Great Escape*, Cassell, 2000

Bowman, Martin, *Nachtjagd*, Defenders of the Reich 1940-1943, Pen & Sword Aviation, 2016

Bowman, Martin, *The Wellington Bomber Story*, The History Press Ltd, 2011

Brown, Malcolm, *Spitfire Summer: When Britain Stood Alone*, Carlton Books, 2000

Bungay, Stephen, *The Most Dangerous Enemy: A History of the Battle of Britain,* Aurum Press, 2015

Carey, John, *The Faber Book of Reportage*, Faber, 1987

Churchill, Winston, *The Second World War, Volume II*, Cassell, 1949

Clutton-Brock, Oliver, *Footprints on the Sands of Time: RAF Bomber Command Prisoners-of-War in Germany 1939-1945*, Grub Street Publishing, 2003

Cull, Brian, *Battle for the Channel: The First Month of the Battle of Britain 10 July – 10 August 1940*, Fonthill Media, 2017

Deighton, Len, *Fighter: The True Story of the Battle of Britain*, Jonathan Cape, 1977

Donnelly, Larry, *The Other Few: Bomber and Coastal Command Operations in the Battle of Britain*, Red Kite, 2014

Ferguson, Norman, *The Battle of Britain: A Miscellany*, Summersdale, 2015

Foot, M.R.D. and Langley, J.M., *MI9: Escape and Evasion 1939–45*, Biteback Publishing, 2011

Franks, Norman, *Royal Air Force Fighter Command Losses of the Second World War, Volume I 1939–41*, Midland Publishing, 2008

Franks, Norman, *Images of War: The RAF Air Sea Rescue Service in the Second World War*, Pen & Sword Aviation, 2016

Galland, Adolf, *The First and the Last*, Methuen, 1955

Gibson, Guy, *Enemy Coast Ahead*, Crecy Classic, 2017

Goss, Chris, *The Luftwaffe Bombers: Battle of Britain*, Crecy Publishing, 2000

Goss, Chris, *Heinkel He111: The Early Years*, Frontline Books, 2017

Goss, Chris, *Knights of the Battle of Britain: Luftwaffe Aircrew Awarded the Knight's Cross in 1940*, Frontline Books, 2018

Green, William, *Aircraft of the Battle of Britain* (2nd revised edition), Jane's Information Group, 1980

Gretzyngier, Robert, *Poles in Defence of Britain*, Grub Street Publishing, 2000

Gustavsson, Hakan and Slongo, Ludovico, *Fiat CR.42 Aces of World War 2*, Osprey Publishing, 2009

Haining, Peter, *The Chianti Raiders*, Robson Books, 2005

Hall, Steve and Quinlan, Lionel, *KG55*, Red Kite, 2000

Hastings, Max, *Bomber Command*, Pan Military Classics, 2010

Hillier, Mark, *The RAF Battle of Britain Fighter Pilot's Kitbag*, Frontline Books, 2018

Holland, James, *The Battle of Britain: Five Months That Changed History*, Corgi, 2011

Joseph, Frank, *Mussolini's War: Fascist Italy's Military Struggles from Africa and Western Europe to the Mediterranean and Soviet Union 1935-45*, Helion & Company, 2010

Kaplan, Philip, *The Few: Preparation for the Battle of Britain: Images of War*, Pen & Sword Aviation, 2014

Laycock, Stuart and Laycock, Philip, *Unexpected Britain: A Journey Through Our Hidden History*, Amberley Publishing, 2015

Leasor, James and Burt, Kendall, *The One That Got Away*, James Leasor Publishing, 2015

Levine, Joshua, *Forgotten Voices of the Blitz and the Battle of Britain*, Ebury Press, 2007

Logolusu, Alfredo, *Fiat CR.32 Aces of the Spanish Civil War*, Osprey Publishing, 2010

Lopez, Jean; Aubin, Nicolas; Barnard, Vincent and Guillerat, Nicolas, *World War II Infographics*, Thames and Hudson, 2019

Massimello, Giovanni and Apostolo, Giorgio, *Italian Aces of World War 2*, Osprey Publishing, 2000

McCutcheon, Campbell (Ed.), *How to Fly a Battle of Britain Fighter*, Amberley Publishing, 2014

McKay, Sinclair, *The Secret Life of Fighter Command*, Aurum Press, 2015

Middlebrook, Martin and Everitt, Chris, *The Bomber Command War Diaries: An Operational Reference Book 1939–1945*, Pen and Sword Aviation, 2014

Mombeek, Eric; Wadman, David and Pegg, Martin: *Battle of Britain: Phase Two, August–September 1940*, Ian Allan Publishing, 2001

Moor, Anthony J. *Detling Airfield: A History 1915-1959*, Amberley Publishing, 2011

Moore, Kate, *The Battle of Britain*, Osprey Publishing in association with the Imperial War Museum, 2010

Ogilvie, Keith C., *You Never Know Your Luck*, Fighting High, 2016

Olson, Lynne, *Last Hope Island,* Scribe, 2018

Overy, Richard, *The Air War 1939–1945*, MW Books, 1980

Overy, Richard, *The Battle of Britain: Myth and Reality*, Penguin, 2000

Overy, Richard, *The Bombing War: Europe 1939–1945*, Allen Lane, 2013

Parry, Simon W., *Battle of Britain Combat Archive, Volumes 1–5*, Red Kite, 2017

Price, Alfred, *Luftwaffe*, Purnell's History of the Second World War, 1969

Rawnsley, C.F. and Wright, Robert, *Night Fighter*, Collins, 1957

Ray, John, *The Battle of Britain: Dowding and the First Victory, 1940*, Cassell Military Paperbacks, 2000

Rollings, Charles, *Wire and Walls: RAF Prisoners of War in Itzehoe, Spangenberg and Thorn 1939–42*, Ian Allan Publishing, 2003

Sarkar, Dilip, *The Spitfire Manual*, Amberley Publishing, 2010

Saunders, Andy, *Arrival of Eagles: Luftwaffe Landings in Britain 1939–1945*, Grub Street Publishing, 2014

Saunders, Andy, *Luftwaffe Bombers in the Battle of Britain,* Pen & Sword Aviation, 2014

Shores, Christopher and Williams, Clive, *Aces High*, Grub Street, 1994

Snow, Dan, *On This Day in History*, John Murray Publishers, 2018

Stoddard, Brooke C., *World in the Balance: The Perilous Months of June-October 1940*, Pontomac Books, 2011

Taylor, A.J.P., *The Second World War: An Illustrated History*, Penguin, 1976

Thomas, Nick, *Their Finest Hour: Stories of the Men who Won the Battle of Britain*, Pen & Sword Aviation, 2016

Thompson, Wing Commander H.L., *New Zealanders with the Royal Air Force (Vol. II)*, part of the Official History of New Zealand in the Second World War 1939–45, Historical Publications Branch, Wellington, 1956

Thorburn, Gordon, *The Squadron That Died Twice: The Story of No. 82 Squadron*, John Blake, 2015

Tuck, Howard and Grehan, Howard, *Stalag Luft III: An Official History of the 'Great Escape' PoW Camp*, Pen & Sword

Vader, John, *Spitfire*, Ballantine's Illustrated History of World War II, 1969

Vasco, John, *Messerschmitt Bf110: Bombsights over England / Erprobungsgruppe 210 in the Battle of Britain*, Schiffer, 2002

Wellum, Geoffrey, *First Light*, Penguin, 2003

Wynn, Kenneth G., *Men of the Battle of Britain: A Biographical Directory of The Few*, Frontline Books in association with the Battle of Britain Memorial Trust, 2015

Acknowledgements

THE GENESIS FOR this book was a lunch with Rupert Lancaster, head of non-fiction at Hodder & Stoughton, during which we tried to find a story that cast new light on the Battle of Britain. In the end, we found eighteen stories – eighteen men, eighteen machines, eighteen missions – that involved many people in the telling.

We are grateful to all those who helped us, or tried to help us, starting with Rupert, his assistant, Cameron Myers, and our literary agents, Mark Lucas and Barbara Levy.

Much of the research was undertaken by Jessica Savage-Hanford, who spent many hours delving into archives and seeking information across the world. We would also like to thank Alex Blair; Tim Bullamore, particularly for his work on the chapter on Wing Commander Edward Lart; Charles Dick, Finn Charlton-Jones and Harold Pearson for their endeavours on our behalf.

We are grateful to the aviation historian Chris Goss, in particular for his advice on sources and his analysis of the battle, and the many authors on whose work we have drawn in order to tell these stories, especially the historians Richard Overy and Max Hastings. We would also like to thank the Curtis Brown Group Ltd, acting on behalf of the Estate of Winston S Churchill, for permission to quote Britain's wartime prime minister.

We would like to say a special thank you to Dave Harvey, a former RAF pilot who is now a volunteer pilot with the Historic Aircraft Collection. He hosted a memorable visit for us at Duxford airfield in Cambridgeshire, where we were given the chance to sit in the cockpits of both a Spitfire and a Hurricane.

Several of the families of the pilots featured in this book helped us. We would like to thank Lynne Florence, the daughter of Flight Lieutenant Neil Svendsen, and his niece Joanne Svendsen; Dr David Jones, the nephew of Pilot Officer W.H.C. 'Clem' Hunkin; John

Lart Jr, the nephew of Wing Commander Edward Lart; Sarah Nicholls, the granddaughter of Squadron Leader Philip Hunter; Keith C. Ogilvie, the son of Squadron Leader Keith 'Skeets' Ogilvie; Adam Tuke, the son of Lieutenant Anthony 'Steady' Tuke; and Wieslaw Wlasnowolski, the nephew of Pilot Officer Boleslaw Wlasnowolski, and other relatives in Poland. We are grateful to Joan Langmead for her recollections of the discovery of PO Wlasnowolski's aircraft and Radek Sikoski for his research suggestions in Poland.

We would like to thank Bee Benton for her help in Deal in researching the chapter on Flight Sergeant Willi Effmert. In New Zealand we would like to thank John King, the editor of *Aviation News, New Zealand*; Simon Moody and Louisa Hormann, research curators at the Air Force Museum of New Zealand; and Peter 'PJ' Montgomery, Georgina Ralston, Denis Aitken and Heather Hore, for their efforts in tracking down details of the life of Flight Lieutenant Russell 'Digger' Aitken.

We also thank Elisabeth Westmore and Johannes Sprenger of the Sylter Archive in Westerland, who corresponded on our behalf with the family of Erich Chudziak.

We would like to thank the staff of the Biggin Hill Memorial Museum, the Imperial War Museum, the National Archives at Kew, the RAF Museum, and the Bundesarchiv in Berlin. We are grateful to historians Paul Beaver and Geoff Simpson and to Melanie Chew, the development director at the Seckford Foundation; Group Captain Patrick Tootal of the Battle of Britain Memorial Trust; Darren Priday of the RAF Museum Cosford; and Lianne May of RDF Television. Thanks also to Kezia Levitas and Sara Rumens for their advice on photographs.

We are also grateful to former colleagues at *The Times*, particularly Nigel Farndale and Emma Tucker, for their generous support.

This book could not have been written without the support and understanding of our two families, the Pearsons and the Gormans. Our thanks go particularly to Jeanna and especially to Fiona, who edited the first draft of our manuscript.

References

Karl Henze

https://books.google.co.uk/books?id=ayoncdaxYkQC&pg=PA217
&lpg=PA217&dq=Major+Karl+Henze&source=bl&ots=rSGUjf
JvXK&sig=23wOzL1IARJZSRI8OkMgKP2tqpE&hl=en&sa=X
&ved=2ahUKEwikv87R30XeAhXHa8AKHU6JCe84ChDoAT
AEegQIBRAB#v=onepage&q=Major%20Karl%20Henze&f=
false.

https://books.google.co.uk/books?id=NfRilR2UQXUC&pg=PA
381&lpg=PA381&dq=karl+Henze+German+airforce&source=bl
&ots=SNPio9QRx_&sig=eOC6pKhesRd_eKZqHEq4VNBmY
pk&hl=en&sa=X&ved=2ahUKEwijgfma44beAhVSPsAKHRjiC
GIQ6AEwD30ECAIQAQ#v=onepage&q=karl%20Henze%20
German%20airforce&f=false.

https://books.google.co.uk/books?id=8e23DAAAQBAJ&pg=PA30
&lpg=PA30&dq=karl+Henze+German+airforce&source=bl&ot
s=XNbDnqcCzp&sig=ItFuhe790BhBclaAHN8boUxempo&hl=
en&sa=X&ved=2ahUKEwi6leev5IbeAhWkJsAKHXmUDvE4
ChDoATAAegQICRAB#v=onepage&q=karl%20Henze%20
German%20airforce&f=false.

https://www.valka.cz/topic/view/49330/Henze-Karl.

W.H.C. 'Clem' Hunkin

https://www.thegazette.co.uk/London/issue/35451/page/664/data.pdf.
https://discovery.nationalarchives.gov.uk/details/r/C14503083.
https://digital.nls.uk/british-military-lists/
archive/96019510?mode=transcription.
https://en.wikipedia.org/wiki/1945_Birthday_Honours.
The National Archive (TNA): AIR 81/1144, AIR 40/1909, WO
208/3242.

Erich Chudziak

http://www.wehrmacht-awards.com/forums/showthread.
  php?t=362321&page=2.
http://forum.12oclockhigh.net/showthread.php?t=413.
http://forum.12oclockhigh.net/archive/index.php?t-17979.html.
http://grabsteine.genealogy.net/tomb.
  php?cem=309&tomb=92&lang=en.

Russell Aitken

https://www.thegazette.co.uk/London/issue/34513/page/3358/
  data.pdf.
http://forum.12oclockhigh.net/showthread.php?t=43125.
https://www.thegazette.co.uk/London/issue/36544/supplement/2583.
http://nzetc.victoria.ac.nz//tm/scholarly/tei-WH2-1RAF-c6.html.
http://nzetc.victoria.ac.nz//tm/scholarly/tei-WH2-1RAF-c10.html.

Edward Collis de Virac Lart

http://www.rafmuseumstoryvault.org.uk/ID/?7000277050.
https://findvej.dk/?longitude=9.5451&latitude=57.1722&zoom=16
  &maptype=3.
https://www.airmen.dk/p022.htm.
https://www.airmen.dk/tranumeng.htm.
https://www.airmen.dk/a107007.htm.
https://www.reddit.com/r/AirForce/comments/7kye9x/death_
  of_a_bomber_squadron/.
https://www.iwm.org.uk/memorials/item/memorial/25311.
https://www.thegazette.co.uk/London/issue/34866/page/3436/
  data.pdf.
https://www.thegazette.co.uk/London/issue/34366/page/717/
  data.pdf.
https://www.thegazette.co.uk/London/issue/33046/page/3224/
  data.pdf.
https://www.unithistories.com/officers/RAF_officers_L01.html.
http://www.roll-of-honour.com/Devon/Newton
  Poppleford.html.

http://www.rafcommands.com/database/wardead/index.
  php?qname=&qcntry=Denmark&cur=0&qunit=82%20
  Sqdn&qnum=&qmem=&qdate=.

https://digital.nls.uk/british-military-lists/archive/ 96067190?mode
  =transcription.

https://da.wikipedia.org/wiki/Allierede_flyvere.

http://aircrewremembered.com/AircrewDeaths39-47/
  aircrewdeaths-alpha-list-l-r.html.

https://www.freshford.com/charmouth_1911_names.htm.

https://www.forces-war-records.co.uk/records/5268242/wing-
  commander-edward-collis-de-viraclart-royal-air-force-82-squadron/.

https://www.scribd.com/document/214623313/Looking-Back-Issue-4.

https://www.cwgc.org/find-war-dead/casualty/2271610/lart,-
  edward-collis-de-virac/.

https://discovery.nationalarchives.gov.uk/details/r/D8454542;
  TNA: AIR 27/681/19, AIR27/681/20.

Walter Rubensdorffer

Boy, Walter J., *Clash of Wings: World War II in the Air*, documentary
  TV series, Discovery Channel

https://ipfs.io/ipfs/QmXoypizjW3WknFiJnKLwHCnL72vedxjQk
  DDP1mXWo6uco/wiki/ Walter_Rubensdörffer.html.

https://www.tracesofwar.com/persons/70975/Rubensdörffer-
  Walter.htm.

https://commons.wikimedia.org/wiki/File:Luftwaffe_collar_tabs_
  Hauptmann_3D.svg.

https://www.456fis.org/ME-210.htm.

https://hystoricus.wordpress.com/tag/raf-vs-luftwaffe/.

https://ww2aircraft.net/forum/.

https://www.wikiwand.com/en/Kanalkampf.

https://epdf.pub/messerschmitt-me-210410.html.

https://www.revolvy.com/page/Kanalkampf.

https://elgrancapitan.org/foro/viewtopic.php?f=52&t=24794.

https://www.pprune.org/archive/index.php/t-115579.html.

https://bg.battletech.com/forums/index.php?topic=57861.0.

https://www.facebook.com/SpitfireHurricaneMemorialMuseum /
  posts/1732587316851304.

https://peoplepill.com/people/walter-rubensdoerffer/.
https://www.youtube.com/watch?v=G4x7F3rT0OY.
https://www.wingsofwar.org/forums/showthread.php?24865-Bf-
    109E-quot-Jabo-quot-with-bombhistorical-scenario.
https://infogalactic.com/info/Battle_of_Britain#Luftwaffe_strategy.
https://forums-de.ubi.com/archive/index.php/t-14419-p-
    994.html.
http://biblioteka.mycity-military.com/biblioteka/cyber%20
    fulkrum/ E%20N%20G%20L%20E%20S%20K%20I/AC%20
    4%20Publication%20i%20drugo/ AC_- _Allied_Fighters.pdf.
http://fileserver.net-texts.com/asset.aspx?dl=no&id=26457.
https://weaponsandwarfare.com/2016/06/16/fighter-bombers-
    against-england/.
https://keepituryens.wordpress.com/2016/08/15/local-rotherfield-
    wartime-history-4-battle-ofbritain-crash-site-erprobungsgruppe-
    210-walter-rubensdorffers-bf110.
http://ww2f.com/threads/erpro-210.9304/.
http://bobgamehub.blogspot.com/p/about-battle.html.
https://www.manstonhistory.org.uk/second-large-attack-manston-
    battle-britain-14th-august-1940/.
https://discovery.nationalarchives.gov.uk/details/r/D8386279.
https://discovery.nationalarchives.gov.uk/details/r/D8410704.

Philip Hunter

http://www.thepeerage.com/p41128.htm.
https://www.tass.gov.uk/2018/04/26/teenage-student-athlete/.
http://munksroll.rcplondon.ac.uk/Biography/Details/2338.
https://discovery.nationalarchives.gov.uk/details/r/D7491639.
https://discovery.nationalarchives.gov.uk/details/r/D7491656.
https://discovery.nationalarchives.gov.uk/details/r/D7491608.
https://discovery.nationalarchives.gov.uk/details/r/D7491642;
    TNA: AIR 50/104/109.

Ernst Wedding

Imperial War Museum: Wedding, Ernest (oral history, 2004),
    catalogue number 26960.

https://www.imdb.com/title/tt1058006/.
https://docuwiki.net/index.php?title=Spitfire_Ace.
https://www.youtube.com/watch?v=t3YiNICve7M.
https://www.youtube.com/watch?v=RUnznl9RiiU.
https://www.youtube.com/watch?v=aHrdCJLLVXU.
https://www.youtube.com/watch?v=GM9b3bbqVdk.
https://www.youtube.com/watch?v=1CMO7WolY5c.

Neil H. Svendsen

http://www.rafcommands.com/forum/showthread.php?21714-P-
    O-later-S-L-Stanley-Carter- (79230)&styleid=3.
https://www.thegazette.co.uk/London/issue/38125/
    supplement/5434/data.pdf.
http://nzetc.victoria.ac.nz/tm/scholarly/tei-WH2-1RAF-
    b8.html.
https://deriv.nls.uk/dcn23/9605/96050345.23.pdf.
https://www.myheritage.com/names/neil_svendsen.
http://www.danishww2pilots.dk/profiles.php?id=232.
http://discovery.nationalarchives.gov.uk/details/r/D8454645.
    TNA: AIR81/2801, AIR81/7281, AIR27/686/4 to
    AIR27/686/38.

Willi Effmert

http://warbirdsnews.com/aviation-museum-news/dornier-17-
    retrieved-goodwin-sands-arrives-raf-museum-cosford.html.
http://forum.12oclockhigh.net/archive/index.php?t-22195.html.
https://www.telegraph.co.uk/history/world-war-two/11655696/
    Last-Dornier-bomber-being-restored-after-being-hidden-for-
    over-70-years.html.
https://www.battleofbritain1940.net/0030.html.
https://www.aeroresource.co.uk/news/rafm-cosford-dornier-do17-
    preservation/.
    TNA: AIR27/317/11, AIR27/317/12.

Baron Franz von Werra

Luftwaffe Officer Career Summaries Section S–Z Version
(updated 2019), by Henry L. de Zeng IV and Douglas G.
Stankey: www.ww2.dk/Lw%20Offz%20-%20S-Z%20-%20
Apr%202019.pdf.

http://hucknallparishchurch.org.uk/franz-von-werra/.

http://www.luftwaffe.cz/werra.html.

http://www.ournottinghamshire.org.uk/page/the_hucknall_incident.

https://www.youtube.com/watch?v=gzlBY4R-NQE.

https://www.warhistoryonline.com/instant-articles/franz-von-
werra-german-pow.html.

http://valourcanada.ca/military-history-library/luftwaffe-pow-
escapes-in-ontario/.

https://ajhydell.com/2019/03/31/german-fighter-ace-baron-franz-
von-werra-the-only-german-to-escape-canadian-captivity-in-
his-cockpit-with-his-pet-lion-simba-germany-1940-795x689/.

https://books.google.co.uk/books?id=IbHADgAAQBAJ&pg=PT
34&lpg=PT34&dq=Baron+FRanz+von+Werra&source=bl&ots
=3dNVZjO68C&sig=ACfU3U0Jw7L7HQqQJRKXtWa3Px
NDlqVoAA&hl=en&sa=X&ved=2ahUKEwj2_4i00IjlAhUJEc
AKHSO7Dqs4RhD0ATAAegQIBxAB#v=onepage&q=Baron
%20FRanz%20von%20Werra&f=false.

Keith Olgivie

https://bhmm.org.uk/collections/explore-the-collections/?eHive_
query=keith%20Ogilvie.

http://www.bbm.org.uk/airmen/Ogilvie.htm.

http://acesofww2.com/can/aces/ogilvie/.

http://www.vintagewings.ca/VintageNews/Stories/tabid/116/
articleType/ArticleView/articleId/595/Gunfight-over-
WestminsterThe-Spitfire-Luck-of-Skeets-Ogilvie.aspx.

https://www.newspapers.com/clip/3898906/ottawa_flyer_keith_
skeets_ogilvie/.

https://www.sherbrookerecord.com/lois-blanchette-remembers-
cousin-recounts-harrowing-tale-of-escape/.

Anthony 'Steady' Tuke

Imperial War Museum: Tuke, Anthony Montague 'Steady' (oral history, 2006), catalogue number 28766: https://www.iwm.org.uk/collections/item/object/80026944.

https://www.telegraph.co.uk/news/obituaries/military-obituaries/naval-obituaries/8002873/ Lieutenant-Commander-Steady-Tuke.html.

http://www.n5490.org/Pilots/Pilots.html.

http://www.n5490.org/Pilots/Tuke/Tuke.html.

https://www.unithistories.com/officers/RN_officersT2.html.

https://chestnut-ah.livejournal.com/424792.html.

https://discovery.nationalarchives.gov.uk/details/r/C2226150; TNA: ADM 207/23 (826 Squadron diary).

Boleslaw Wlasnowolski

http://encyklopedia.naukowy.pl/ Bolesław_Własnowolski#Przypisy

https://www.altair.com.pl/magazines/article?article_id=4018.

https://www.tracesofwar.com/persons/49185/Wlasnowolski-Boreslaw-Andrzej.htm?c=aw.

http://forum.12oclockhigh.net/archive/index.php?t-31660.html.

https://military.wikia.org/wiki/Bajan%27s_list.

http://aces.safarikovi.org/victories/lista.bajana.pdf.

https://www.samoloty.pl/ludzie-lotnictwa-hobby-1807/zwipzani-z-lotnictwem-hobby-1809/polscyhobby-2191/wasnowolski-bolesaw.

http://dictionnaire.sensagent.leparisien.fr/122%20Eskadra%20Myśliwska/pl-pl/.

http://www.polishsquadronsremembered.com/308/308_part1.html.

http://www.historycy.org/historia/index.php/t13051.html.

https://www.geograph.org.uk/photo/9297.

https://niebieskaeskadra.pl/?control=8&id=4540.

http://www.klub-beskid.com/phorum/read.php?16,258158.

https://www.ebay.pl/itm/ASY-polskiego-lotnictwa-Zieli-ski-ACES-Polish-aviation-ASSEpolnischen-Luftfahrt-/351652858413.

https://www.youtube.com/watch?v=8xM6t8gJzuc.

http://pub.wolnosc.net/INTERNET2000/Mysliwcy/1939/122_
   eskadra_mysliwska.htm.
http://www.muzeumlotnictwa.pl/index.php/aktualnosci/
   szczegoly/193/280;
TNA: AIR50/170/49.

Fritz Ruhlandt

http://www.kentfallen.com/PDF%20reports/GRAVENEY.pdf.
http://jewelencrustedpisspot.co.uk/TimeGun/last
   _battle.html.
https://www.feldgrau.net/forum/viewtopic.php?t=30001.
http://www.wwiireenacting.co.uk/forum/viewtopic.
   php?f=1&t=55457.
https://www.pressreader.com.
https://www.kentonline.co.uk/kent/news/forgotten-frontline-
   exhibition-t-a93111/.
http://st.louis.irish.tripod.com.
https://www.dailymail.co.uk/news/article-1304704/Graveney-
   Marsh-Last-Battle-Britain-finallyremembered-70
   -years.html.
http://spitfiresite.com/2010/10/battle-of-britain-1940-graveney-
   marsh.html.
https://weaponsandwarfare.com/2016/08/31/the-battle-of-
   graveney-marsh/.
https://histmag.org/Ostatnia-bitwa-na-brytyjskiej-ziemi-czyli-
   historia-pewnej-legendy-10824.
https://www.blogger.com/
   blogin.g?blogspotURL=http%3A%2F%2Fmagiahistorii.blogspot.
   com%2F2015%2F03%2Fostatnia-bitwana-brytyjskiej-ziemi.
   html&bpli=1.
http://overlord-wot.blogspot.com/2013/09/the-real-operation-
   sealion_8.html.
https://discovery.nationalarchives.gov.uk/details/r/C790494;
   TNA: WO166/4435.

Giuseppe Ruzzin

https://www.mursia.com/index.php/it/storia/ali-daquila-detail

http://surfcity.kund.dalnet.se/italy_ruzzin.htm.

http://ww2f.com/threads/giuseppe-ruzzin-italian-ace.19916/.

http://www.eaf51.org/newweb/Documenti/Storia/Ruzzin.pdf.

https://www.pinterest.co.uk/pin/310185493066495439/.

https://en.wikipedia.org/wiki/List_of_World_War_II_aces_from_
Italy.

http://www.ww2wings.com/wings/spain/legionariapilot.shtml.

https://www.suter-meggen.ch/ bausaetze/italeri/sortiment/
detailseiten/italeri_2719.php.

http://www.storiainrete.com/7133/storia-militare/elica-e-littorio-
per-combattere-una-guerra-tuttain-picchiata/.

http://www.ww2incolor.com/italian-forces/BF109-CAI-2.html.

http://www.alieuomini.it/AJAX/catalogo/dettaglio2_
catalogo/106/.

https://www.valka.cz/10806-Corpo-Aereo-Italiano-v-Bitke-o-
Britaniu.

https://miles.forumcommunity.net/?t=54230211.

http://www.flyinglions.eu/storia/aviazione/item/261-3-gruppo-
ct-della-regia-aeronautica.html.

http://win.storiain.net/arret/num159/artic7.asp.

https://www.asisbiz.com/Battles/ANR-Battle-of-Britain.html.

https://discovery.nationalarchives.gov.uk/details/r/D7441141.

https://discovery.nationalarchives.gov.uk/details/r/D7445190;
TNA: AIR 50/20/76.

Arthur Hodgkinson

http://www.bbm.org.uk/airmen/Hodgkinson.htm.

https://www.cwgc.org/find-war-dead/casualty/2373234/
hodgkinson,-arthur-john/.

https://en.wikipedia.org/wiki/List_of_RAF_aircrew_in_the_
Battle_of_Britain_(G–K).

http://www.oldhaltonians.co.uk/pages/rememb/gall/gall02.htm.

https://www.historynet.com/aviation-history-book-review-
beaufighter-aces-world-war-2.htm.

http://www.626-squadron.co.uk/willem4.htm.

https://discovery.nationalarchives.gov.uk/details/r/D7444295.

https://discovery.nationalarchives.gov.uk/details/r/C1912613.

https://discovery.nationalarchives.gov.uk/details/r/D8394412;
   TNA: AIR50/84/23, AIR50/84/38, AIR50/8440,
   AIR50/84/41, AIR50/84/42.

Bernhard Jope

Luftwaffe Officer Career Summaries Section G–K (updated
   2019), by Henry L. de Zeng IV and Douglas G. Stankey:
   www.ww2.dk/Lw%20Offz%20-%20G-K%20-%20Apr%
   202019.pdf.

https://books.google.co.uk/books?id=T7OhDAAAQBAJ&pg=P
   A21&lpg=PA21&dq=bernhard+jope&source=bl&ots=4GfG
   wKMV-6&sig=Luv5A7y8894KoLC3AmBlGC9QooI&hl=en&s
   a=X&ved=2ahUKEwjHoNuLq-XeAhXJJMAKHR1JBnA4Ch
   DoATALegQIARAB#v=onepage&q=bernhard%20
   jope&f=false.

https://www.tracesofwar.com/persons/23585/Jope-Bernhard.
   htm?c=aw.

http://ww2today.com/26th-october-1940-empress-of-britain-
   bombed-at-sea.

http://dir.md/wiki/Bernhard_Jope?host=en.wikipedia.org.

https://forum.axishistory.com/viewtopic.php?t=72875.

https://play.google.com/books/reader?id=T7OhDAAAQBAJ&
   printsec=frontcover&source=gbs_atb_hover&pg=GBS.PP1.

https://en.wikipedia.org/wiki/Focke-Wulf_Fw_200_Condor.

http://ww2today.com/august-1940-condor-aircraft-join-the-battle-
   of-the-atlantic.

Files on German prisoners of war

The National Archives, Kew. TNA: WO208, FO1050/169,
   AIR40/2394, ADM186/806–809, CO968/35/1.

General

As noted in the Acknowledgements, biographical material, letters and records were supplied to the authors by several of the families of the pilots featured in this book, including Lynne Florence, the daughter of Flight Lieutenant Neil Svendsen, and his niece Joanne Svendsen; Dr David Jones, the nephew of Pilot Officer W.H.C. 'Clem' Hunkin; John Lart Jr, nephew of Wing Commander Edward Lart; Sarah Nicholls, the granddaughter of Squadron Leader Philip Hunter; Keith C. Ogilvie, the son of Squadron Leader Keith 'Skeets' Ogilvie; Adam Tuke, the son of Lieutenant Anthony 'Steady' Tuke; and Wieslaw Wlasnowolski, nephew of Pilot Officer Boleslaw Wlasnowolski, and other relatives in Poland.

The Battle of Britain Historical Society: https://www. battleofbritain1940.net/contents-index.html.

Picture Acknowledgements

Courtesy AircrewRemembered.com: 5 above, 13 above. Courtesy Air Force Museum of New Zealand: 30 (Creative Commons BY-NC/Image file 2006/715.1i). akg-images/Sammlung Berliner Verlag/Archive: 22. Courtesy The Battle of Britain London Monument: 184. BBC Motion Gallery/Getty Images: 81 centre. Bundesarchive: 25 above (Bild 101I-342-0612-02A/Foto Jütte), 103 above (Bild 101I-341-0481-39A/Foto Spieth), 103 below (Bild 101I-341-0456-04/Foto Folkerts), 193 below left (Bild 146-1978-043-02/Foto o.Ang). Courtesy Lynne Florence (née Svendsen): 84, 89 above left. Getty Images: xvi, 5 below, 13 centre, 36, 58 below, 69 below left, 74, 81 above, 89 centre and below, 98, 108,115 above, 128 centre and below, 169, 193 centre. © Ed Gorman: 146. Chris Goss: 188, 193 above right. © Imperial War Museum London: 58 above (CH 15183), 64 (CH 885), 69 centre (CH 196), 81 below C 5422), 142 above right (A 29005), 142 below (A 10657), 152 above left (HU 54510), 152 centre right (HU 2408), 160 above (H 6351). Courtesy Dr David Jones: 10, 13 below. Courtesy John Lart: 38, 49 centre and below. Courtesy Sarah Nicholls (née Hunter): 69 above left. Collection of Keith Ogilvie: 118, 128 above left. Private collections: 49 above, 134, 152 below, 164. © The Royal Aeronautical Society (National Aerospace Library)/Mary Evans Picture Library: 115 below, 174. © Andy Saunders: 156, 160 centre left and below. John Vasco via Chris Goss 52. Wilkes/Dannenberg/Jessel: Unseren Gefallen. Gedenkbuch der evangelisch-lutherischen Kirchengemeinde Sankt Nicolai in Westerland, 1939-1945 (Sylter Archiv): 25 below. Courtesy Woodbridge School: 142 above left.

Every reasonable effort has been made to trace copyright holders, but if there are any errors or omissions, Hodder & Stoughton will be pleased to insert the appropriate acknowledgement in any subsequent printings or editions.

Index